Jade Christine Angelica, MDiv

We Are Not Alone
A Teenage Boy's Personal Account of Child Sexual Abuse from Disclosure Through Prosecution and Treatment

Pre-publication
REVIEWS,
COMMENTARIES,
EVALUATIONS . . .

"In *We Are Not Alone*, Jade Christine Angelica provides a valuable resource to teens who have been sexually abused and their parents. With compassion and eloquent prose, she walks people through the criminal justice system—from disclosure to final outcome. I believe that her book will be a lifeline to families of teens who have disclosed sexual abuse."

Kathleen Kendall-Tackett, PhD
Research Associate,
Family Research Laboratory,
University of New Hampshire,
Durham

"*We Are Not Alone* is a must read for all who work or live with kids who have been abused. It explores abuse through the eyes of the victims, sharing their fears, hopes, and wishes. It inspires us to work harder to meet kids' needs, answer their questions, calm their fears, and protect them from their abusers and a system that is often not designed to respond to them in a language they understand.

We Are Not Alone highlights the fact that to those of us who work with abused kids, it is our job; but to the kids, it is their life. We must never forget that. *We Are Not Alone* helps us realize that we are also not alone, and that is a great thing. We must all work together to end abuse, and this wonderful book offers tremendous insights into kids and how best to achieve that goal."

Kevin L. Ryle, JD
Assistant District Attorney,
Middlesex, Massachusetts

More pre-publication
REVIEWS, COMMENTARIES, EVALUATIONS . . .

"**I** have the utmost gratitude and praise for Jade Christine Angelica's *We Are Not Alone* guidebook and companion workbooks. They are long-awaited comprehensive and compelling resources for victims and families involved in the child protection and criminal justice systems and the many professionals who work to assist and support them. As a professional working in victim services for almost twenty years, I know how complex and intimidating the system is for victims of all ages and their families. It is particularly daunting for children and adolescents, since the criminal justice system was not designed to meet their unique physical, emotional, and developmental needs. The guidebook points out the harsh realities of the system, but also clearly and sensitively highlights the strides that the child protection and criminal justice systems have made over the past two decades and the efforts to prevent those systems from re-victimizing those they seek to protect. True, the systems are complicated to navigate, but the author is extremely successful in demystifying the system and informing the reader of the positive ways in which the system can and does respond. She strongly encourages victims and their families to participate in the system in an effort to heal from their victimization, seek justice, and hold offenders accountable for their heinous and harmful crimes.

The guidebook is useful not only for victims and their families, but also for professionals working with teen victims and participating as members of multidisciplinary teams. With high staff turnover in many of the agencies involved, this is an exceedingly vital training tool as well. And, of course, the workbooks provide the means by which to engage adolescents in their own care—supporting them in the aftermath of their victimization, helping them engage in quiet introspection, guiding their interactions and conversations with helping professionals and family members, and assisting them to gain the courage necessary to participate in the criminal justice system. Ultimately, these publications will enable them to achieve the goals of vindication, justice, and healing."

Janet E. Fine, MS
Director,
Victim Witness Assistance Program
and Children's Advocacy Center,
Suffolk County District Attorney's Office,
Boston

HMTP

The Haworth Maltreatment and Trauma Press®
An Imprint of The Haworth Press, Inc.
New York • London • Oxford

We Are Not Alone

A Teenage Boy's Personal Account of Child Sexual Abuse from Disclosure Through Prosecution and Treatment

We Are Not Alone
A Teenage Boy's Personal Account of Sexual Abuse from Disclosure Through Prosecution and Treatment

Jade Christine Angelica, MDiv

HMTP

The Haworth Maltreatment and Trauma Press®
An Imprint of The Haworth Press, Inc.
New York • London • Oxford

Published by

The Haworth Maltreatment and Trauma Press®, an imprint of The Haworth Press, Inc., 10 Alice Street, Binghamton, NY 13904-1580

PUBLISHER'S NOTE
All of the characters in the *We Are Not Alone* workbooks are fictitious. Any resemblance to actual persons, living or dead, or events in their lives, is entirely coincidental.

Cover design by Jennifer M. Gaska.

Library of Congress Cataloging-in-Publication Data

Angelica, Jade C. (Jade Christine), 1952-
We are not alone: a teenage boy's personal account of child sexual abuse from disclosure through prosecution and treatment / Jade Christine Angelica.
p. cm.
ISBN 0-7890-0927-7 (soft : alk. paper)
1. Child sexual abuse. 2. Sexually abused children. 3. Sexually abused children—Mental health. 4. Trials (Child sexual abuse) I. Title.

HV6570 .A544 2002
364.15'36—dc21
[B]
                                                                              2001016622

For Steve,

You are an inspiration.

ABOUT THE AUTHOR

Jade Christine Angelica, MDiv, Director of The Child Abuse Ministry, has been working on behalf of victims of child sexual abuse since 1987. A graduate of Harvard Divinity School, Ms. Angelica leads workshops and training sessions for religious leaders and communities, develops programs and conferences, preaches, lectures, and writes on the topic of child sexual abuse. From 1989 to 1993, Ms. Angelica researched and developed special projects for the Child Abuse Unit of the Middlesex County District Attorney's Office in Cambridge, Massachusetts. In order to provide a sorely needed court-oriented resource for adolescent victims of child sexual abuse, Ms. Angelica wrote the first edition of *We Are Not Alone: A Teenage Girl's Personal Account of Incest Through Prosecution and Treatment,* which was printed in 1992 with a grant from the Massachusetts Bar Association.

Also during her time at the Child Abuse Unit, Ms. Angelica realized the importance of involving faith communities and religious leaders in the multidisciplinary efforts of prevention and healing of child sexual abuse. She is also the author of *A Moral Emergency: Breaking the Cycle of Child Sexual Abuse,* a handbook for religious leaders.

CONTENTS

Introduction   1
       Renee Brant

Welcome to the Teen Reader   3

Identification of Characters   5

Section 1. I'm Joe   7

Section 2. The First Time I Told   9

Section 3. I'm Sorry   13

Section 4. Making a Report   15

Section 5. The Investigation Begins   17

Section 6. The Interview   19

Section 7. After the Interview   21

Section 8. Counseling   25

Section 9. Prosecution Begins   29

Section 10. Pretrial Testimony   31

Section 11. Counseling Support   33

Section 12. Waiting   35

Section 13. At School   37

Section 14. The Indictment   39

Section 15. The Arraignment   41

Section 16. Waiting Again   43

Section 17. The Empty Courtroom   45

Section 18. Pretrial Details   47

Section 19. Delays and Preparations   49

Section 20. The Trial Begins   51

Section 21. In Court   53

Section 22. Cross-Examination   55

Section 23. Instructions to the Jury   57

Section 24. The Verdict   59

Section 25. After the Trial   61

Section 26. Victim Impact Statement   63

Section 27. Sentencing   65

Section 28. Toward Recovery   69

Section 29. Guiding Questions   71

Support People I Can Depend On   79

How It Happened For Me: A Diagram   80

Glossary   81

Introduction

Renee Brant

I am honored to introduce you to *We Are Not Alone*, a sensitive rendering of a teenage boy's experience in the criminal justice system. You will soon meet Joe, a sixteen-year-old boy who was sexually abused by his neighbor and boys' club leader. In the wake of his disclosure Joe meets many professionals. Each has a role to play in the complicated drama that unfolds as Joe tells school administrators and protective service personnel what happened, begins therapy, and winds his way through the criminal justice process.

The author, Jade Angelica, based Joe's saga on the accounts of many teenagers who generously shared their experiences with her. A "child-friendly" and healing spirit permeates *We Are Not Alone*, and I commend Ms. Angelica for her remarkable capacity to empathize with and learn from the teenagers she interviewed. She translated their experiences into a most readable narrative. In addition, *We Are Not Alone* provides examples from actual encounters with dedicated professionals who labor daily on the "front lines" offering protection, comfort, therapy, support, and legal representation to victimized children and their families.

Contact between children and teenagers and the criminal justice system increased significantly in Massachusetts in 1983 following the passage of the new Child Abuse Reporting Law. This law required the Department of Social Services to report certain cases of severe child abuse and child sexual assault to the district attorney's office. As a result, a tremendous influx of cases involving child and

---

Renee Brant, MD, is the founder of the Sexual Abuse Treatment Team, Children's Hospital, Boston, and is in private practice in child and adolescent psychiatry in Newton, Massachusetts.

teenage victims poured into the criminal justice system. The unique needs of young victims challenged professionals working within the system. These professionals rose to this challenge by developing specialized, interdisciplinary child abuse protection teams and units such as the Middlesex County Child Abuse Division within the Family Protection Unit of the District Attorney's Office.

The people and systems interacting with sexually abused children have a significant impact on these young victims. Those professionals involved in child abuse investigation, protection, and prosecution can become a part of the problem if they are insensitive to the needs of child and teen victims and their families. In Joe's case, however, the child-friendly and knowledgeable helping professionals he met played a significant role in his healing and recovery. Nothing can undo the trauma of child sexual abuse. However, victimized children and adolescents can have a contrasting and profoundly healing experience in relationships with adults when the adults are attentive to the victims' needs, protective of their vulnerabilities, empathetic to their feelings, and validating of their experiences. Thus, in the best of circumstances, professionals can offer child and adolescent victims a trustworthy, respectful relationship which can help them overcome the isolation, shame, and stigma of sexual abuse.

We Are Not Alone serves multiple purposes. It is a resource for teenagers who are facing the unknowns of the criminal justice system. It provides a guide that introduces teenagers to the key players and procedures of the legal process, and a map for them to follow as they travel through the justice system. It also offers teenagers a peer, Joe, with whose thoughts, feelings, and reactions they can identify.

The central message of *We Are Not Alone* is its title. Teenagers reading this book will hopefully experience connections on various levels. They will learn about the network of professionals who are available to help and support them, and they will have a means of identifying with other teenagers who have traveled this difficult road. Through Joe's experiences, teenagers who have been sexually abused will find a path to realizing and understanding their own feelings and perceptions. They will find a comfort in knowing that "we are not alone."

Welcome to the Teen Reader

Dear Reader,

We Are Not Alone was written specifically for teenagers who have been sexually abused and are involved in the prosecution process. However, adults—including parents, relatives, therapists and social workers, doctors, lawyers, judges and other legal professionals, ministers, priests and rabbis, teachers and school administrators—will also find this resource book informative and helpful in their efforts to support and guide teenage victims of child sexual abuse. If you would like supportive adults in your life to have more information about what you are experiencing in the court system, please ask them to read this book.

We Are Not Alone describes the step-by-step process that Joe, a teenager who was sexually abused by his neighbor, experienced in the Massachusetts Superior Court System. On page 80, "How It Happened for Me: A Diagram," illustrates a "typical" superior court process. This diagram should be used only as a guideline, because the actual court process will vary from case to case. The legal process and the support systems will also vary from place to place. Each state and county develops and implements its procedures based on particular needs and available resources. Therefore, try to use *We Are Not Alone* as a springboard for helping you understand how the systems operate in your county or state.

Some of the words and phrases used in the legal system may be unfamiliar to you. Therefore, a **glossary,** which begins on page 81, has been included. Definitions of the words and phrases found in **bold type** within the text are listed alphabetically in the glossary.

As well as describing the legal process, *We Are Not Alone* highlights some of the feelings and reactions experienced by teenagers who are involved in legal proceedings. Not all teenagers will experience things in the exact way Joe does. Again, his feelings and reactions represent the "typical." Actual feelings and reactions will vary according to each individual. At the end of the book is a section of

guiding questions. This section is divided by chapter. Thinking about and answering these questions may help you identify and better understand your own feelings and reactions.

Joe's personal account of child sexual abuse, from disclosure through prosecution and treatment, can be read like a novel, from beginning to end. Or, you may prefer to read only the parts that are of particular interest to you. Each chapter title describes the information covered in that chapter so you can easily locate topics of specific interest.

Joe expresses some intense emotions. Therefore, the account of his experience may be difficult and upsetting to read at times. If it becomes too distressing, put the book down for awhile. You can always come back to it later. But even if it is hard, do try to keep reading at your own pace. Having details and accurate information about the legal system will make the difficult process seem less overwhelming and less frightening.

In many ways, Joe's account presents an idealistic scenario of what happens after a child or a teenager discloses details of sexual abuse. Some child and teen victims who have been sexually abused do find support from their families just as Joe does. However, not all victims are so fortunate. The legal system is designed to provide some support—so young victims do not feel all alone—but it is important for victims to also seek the additional support of relatives, friends, other caring adults, and a qualified therapist.

We Are Not Alone is the result of observations of and interviews with professionals in the legal, victim witness, and mental health fields, as well as conversations with and observations of teen victims of sexual abuse and their families. Although Joe's account is fictitious, the spirit of the actual victims and the helping professionals he meets is alive in this narrative.

My goal in researching and writing *We Are Not Alone* was to help people learn about child sexual abuse and the legal system. I had no idea that being in the presence of children and teenagers who had been sexually abused and their families would teach me invaluable and life-changing lessons. It has been an honor for me to be with you all.

Identification of Characters

Bob: Joe's neighbor and youth club leader. He was accused of sexually abusing Joe.

Mr. Burger: The district attorney on *Perry Mason,* the television show.

Dr. Catherine Clayton (Cathy): Joe's therapist.

Dan: Joe's high school friend.

Dave: Joe's friend in his physical education class.

Ms. Feldman: Joe's high school guidance counselor.

Joy: Joe's high school friend.

Andrew Kane (Drew): The victim witness advocate from the district attorney's office who worked with Joe and his family throughout the prosecution process.

Lisa Lance-White: The child interview specialist from the district attorney's office who met with Joe and conducted the investigative interviews.

Mr. McCarthy: The defense attorney for Bob.

Patrick O'Neill (Pat): The DSS (Department of Social Services) social worker who investigated Joe's disclosure of sexual abuse.

Detective Anthony Rapucci: The local police officer who was part of the team that investigated the allegations against Bob.

Nina Santiago: The assistant district attorney who was in charge of prosecuting the case against Bob.

Mr. Stone: Joe's physical education teacher. The first person Joe told about the sexual abuse.

Section 1

I'm Joe

I'm Joe. I'm sixteen years old, and a junior in high school. I was sexually abused when I was a kid by someone who I thought was my very best friend.

Bob moved into my neighborhood when I was eight. He bought the house on the corner and right away started fixing up his basement. Lots of guys from the neighborhood would hang around on Saturdays and watch him. Sometimes he'd let us help with small stuff like sawing and pounding nails. He built an awesome "rec room" with a pool table, pinball machine, a big-screen TV for video games, and a bar with a Budweiser sign that lit up. He even had an old-fashioned jukebox and lots of old records. We used to give him a hard time about being an "oldie but a goodie." In the spring, we talked Bob into being a youth leader for our neighborhood club. We figured that way we would get to see him more often.

Bob was about forty and divorced. He used to always say how much he missed his family, and that being around the guys made him feel better. My mom said she thought it was strange that Bob didn't seem to have a woman friend, because Mom thought he was handsome and very nice. But Bob said he worked too much and didn't have time for women. I never knew what Bob worked too much doing, but he wore a suit, carried a black briefcase, and took the bus downtown every weekday.

Sometimes the guys would go over to his house on weeknights, especially after the Jefferson Avenue Neighborhood Club meetings. But mostly we went over on Saturdays. Being with Bob was always fun. We played games and goofed around and talked. Bob was great. He was someone I could really talk to. My dad worked downtown, too, and he was usually pretty tired when he came home. But Bob was never too tired for me. Bob was like a friend, and he was like a dad, too. Bob always had time for all the guys. He took us places, bought us presents, and gave us a place to just "hang out."

The refrigerator and cabinets in Bob's rec room were always overflowing with candy and snacks. On Saturdays he would make a special trip to the store and buy whatever we wanted to eat. It became a contest: Who could come up with the grossest snack food? Sometimes Bob gave us money. He said we could buy food and cassette tapes and games with the money if we wanted to, and we could bring them over to share.

One Saturday morning, I noticed a dirty magazine on the bar. I checked it out and then showed it to the other guys. When Bob saw what we were up to, he acted a little strange. He said some grown-up friends had been over the night before and the magazine had been left out by accident. He took it away from me. But about a month later, more magazines showed up. From then on, Bob started to get physical with us. Only at his house, though. Never at our neighborhood club meetings. He was like a different guy at the meetings. You know, distant. And then at home he was so friendly and warm.

Bob said he was teaching us about sex so we would be prepared for dating. He said learning about sex was for our own good. It went on for years, and Bob made us promise never to tell anyone about our "private club," and especially never to tell about our "activities."

I liked the attention Bob gave me, and the sex part felt really good sometimes. I was almost thirteen when I stopped going to Bob's. I don't remember why I stopped, but I just did. I was confused and really depressed because Bob and I couldn't be friends anymore. I missed him. I missed all the fun we had. But I kept my promise. I didn't tell . . . for what seemed like a long, long time I didn't tell. But then I did.

Section 2

The First Time I Told

I still don't know why I told Mr. Stone, my ninth grade physical education teacher. It was early November, and my class was outside running track. Mr. Stone was talking to us about something, and all of a sudden it was like I wasn't there anymore. I was remembering riding by Bob's house on Saturday with my dad. It was like there was this video playing in my head. I saw a bunch of little kids, eight and nine-year-old guys, from around the neighborhood at Bob's. They were getting into the back of his van. Then I realized I couldn't hear what Mr. Stone was saying anymore. His mouth was moving, but I didn't hear any sounds. I started to feel sick to my stomach and dizzy. My head ached. I must have looked dazed, or something, because Dave, the guy next to me, elbowed me and asked if I was okay. I didn't answer him, but just turned away, and started walking across the football field. I don't know where I was going. Dave came after me. He kept asking what was wrong. I kept walking.

Then Mr. Stone came running after me. "Joe. Joe." He was calling to me. It sounded like his voice was calling from a tunnel, all hollow and echoey. He finally caught up to me and put his hand on my shoulder. His touch startled me out of my daze.

Mr. Stone was taller than me, and he had to bend down so he could see into my eyes. "Joe," he said, "What is it? Can I help you?"

I couldn't answer at first. I looked from his face to the ground. I shuffled my feet around, and then, I don't know why, but I just kind of blurted it out. "I was molested by Bob." For a minute after I said it, everything seemed so quiet and still I thought for sure the world had ended. But it didn't. I was still there. Mr. Stone was still there.

Then I kind of started to cry. Mr. Stone just kept saying, "It's okay, Joe. It's okay." He put his arm around me, but that felt horrible to me. I don't know why it felt so bad because Mr. Stone was really nice. But I managed to squirm away from his arm without saying how bad it

9

felt. He maybe understood even if I didn't because he didn't touch me again.

We sat on the field for awhile. I was nervously pulling at the grass, twisting it in my hands, and tossing it into the air. Finally Mr. Stone asked, "Joe, who is Bob?"

"He was my neighbor and the youth leader for the Jefferson Avenue Club," I said. "Bob was my best friend . . . the little guys I saw at his house . . . they looked so small and helpless . . . I wonder why Bob isn't my friend anymore . . . Oh no." I covered my face with my hands and started to cry. I didn't want to cry, but I couldn't stop it. The tears seeped through my fingers. He could see me crying, I just knew it.

Mr. Stone talked to me very quietly and calmly. He said it was okay to cry. He said guys my age had all kinds of thoughts and emotions going on all the time, and we needed to cry sometimes. But, I felt ashamed, anyway. I wished I could sink into the ground and disappear from this place. I didn't want anyone to see me. I didn't want the other guys to know I was crying. I mean, how embarrassing. I especially didn't want anyone to know about me and Bob. What would all the kids say about me? Why did I tell Mr. Stone? Oh no, why did I tell when I promised Bob I wouldn't?

Mr. Stone called Dave over and asked him to tell the class to "hit the showers" and wait in the locker room for the bell. After the guys left, Mr. Stone and I walked into the school building and went to the counseling office. I kept staring at the ground and didn't say a word. I was upset about Bob, for sure, and confused about what he did . . . about what I did. Almost like he could read my mind, Mr. Stone said I did the right thing by telling him about Bob. He said I was brave. It was nice of him to be encouraging, but really, I was so ashamed about making such a scene at school, and so angry at myself for breaking my promise to Bob, that I wasn't feeling "brave."

My guidance counselor, Ms. Feldman, was able to see me right away. It was nice of Mr. Stone to stay around; since he was the first person I told, I just sort of needed him to be there with me. Mr. Stone explained that my high school had standard procedures about how to handle a **disclosure** of sexual abuse and that Ms. Feldman would call the principal, who came quickly to the guidance office after he was called. I felt embarrassed about all the attention I was getting from these adults . . . for such a terrible reason, besides. And I sort of felt like I must be in a lot of trouble because the principal was there. They all assured me that I was not in trouble and I didn't do anything wrong. Ms. Feldman said that telling about what happened with Bob was "right," not "wrong" in any sense.

Since Bob was our youth leader, as well as being my neighbor and friend, the principal said he was in the role of "caretaker." And he said that the commonwealth has a **mandated reporting law,** and a report needed to be filed with the **Department of Social Services (DSS).** "But," the principal said, "I think I should notify your parents first, if you feel okay about me doing that." I nodded. And so, he called my parents. He told my mom and dad it was an emergency, and asked them to come to school right away. Dad wasn't able to leave work, but Mom arrived about thirty minutes later. I waited for her in Ms. Feldman's office. I was really nervous. Ms. Feldman and Mr. Stone and the principal were totally super to me. But I was too upset and confused to be consoled by much of anything.

Section 3

I'm Sorry

Mom arrived to find me sitting in Ms. Feldman's office, staring at the floor, bending and unbending the paper cup I held in my hands. Mom right away said she was worried and confused about this emergency especially because she didn't know what it was all about. When she saw the principal, she asked me if I was in some kind of trouble.

Ms. Feldman answered her question. "No, Joe's not in any trouble. But today during his P.E. class, Joe told Mr. Stone that he had been sexually molested by Bob, his neighbor and youth leader." I was looking up at Mom from the corner of my eye. I realized how important it was for me that my parents believed me.

I could tell Mom was genuinely shocked when she said, "What? Bob?"

She looked at me, and I nodded. "I'm sorry, Mom," I mumbled.

Mom started to cry. "Oh no, Joe," she said. "I'm so sorry. I never should have let you spend so much time with him. But he seemed like such a nice man, and so dedicated to you boys."

The principal continued the discussion. "Our school has procedures in place for handling the disclosure of sexual abuse. Since Mr. Stone is a **mandated reporter,** we are required by law to file an official report with DSS." Then the principal told Mom it was important for my family to be supportive of me, particularly if we intended to follow through with prosecution.

I don't think I've ever seen my mom react so quickly. She jumped out of her chair, and was almost yelling, "Of course we intend to prosecute!" Then she asked to use the phone to call my father. I felt so relieved and grateful . . . Mom believed me.

Dad managed to get away from work when he heard what the emergency was about. He was so mad that I heard him yell, "What?

Bob did what?" through the telephone receiver. Dad arrived at school within the hour.

Dad was really upset, I could tell because his face was red and his forehead was wrinkled. Mom was crying, and I was still staring at the floor. What a scene. But, you know, in spite of all the upset and confusion, I must admit, it was a relief to have let out the secret.

I still felt kind of sad and guilty about telling on Bob, though. I didn't want him to get into any trouble. I loved Bob. He was my friend.

Section 4

Making a Report

While Mr. Stone and the principal were filing the report with DSS over the telephone, my guidance counselor, Ms. Feldman, explained some things to my parents and me about what would happen next. Even though I couldn't look at her, and couldn't really even listen to her, she explained anyway.

Ms. Feldman told us that once a report was received and evaluated a **social worker** would be assigned to my case. Then DSS would have ten days to investigate. Although they legally had ten days to investigate, Ms. Feldman said that a social worker might be in touch with us sooner.

She said that the next several days could be particularly stressful for me. Then she gave me this telephone number for a twenty-four-hour **crisis line,** "just in case" I needed to talk to someone. Like I wanted anyone else to know about this! I was embarrassed enough now that Mr. Stone, Ms. Feldman, the principal, and my parents knew. I mean, what was going to happen when the kids at school found out? They would think I was some weird pervert; I just knew it. And probably none of the other guys from Bob's would want to hang around with me anymore. They would think I was a snitch. And I was sure no one would want to go out on dates with me because I was abused and damaged. This was a terrible mess I'd gotten into.

I wanted to disappear, or run away maybe . . . go someplace new, change my name and start over. But instead, I went home with Mom and Dad, knowing that the DSS social worker would call in a few days to schedule a meeting with me.

When we got home, I went right to my room and turned on a CD—loud! I was trying to drown out Dad's yelling downstairs. He was so mad. I was so ashamed and so scared and so confused. I just sat and stared out the window, tapping my fingers on my desk. After all Bob had done for me, I still couldn't believe I had betrayed him. I didn't know what I was going to do, what was going to happen. I felt like I was being torn in two. Part of me felt so relieved that I had told. Part of me wished I had never said a word.

I was very tense, and when Mom called me for dinner a couple hours later, I almost jumped out of my chair. We ate dinner. No one said anything. Except for the quiet, everything at home seemed just the same as usual. And everything was the same, except inside of me. I was different inside. I knew that it was important for me to let people know about Bob because I just could not get the picture of all those little guys in his van out of my mind. I was scared about what was going to happen next, but I was sad, too. I remembered how much I loved Bob, and how much I thought he loved me. Bob had a way of making me feel so special.

After dinner that night I met a bunch of guys and played basketball for awhile. At first I tried to watch TV, but I was too nervous to sit still, and I knew I had to move around. Basketball was good, but boxing would've been better. I wanted to punch Bob right in the face. Why did he do this to me? When I got home that night I started to cry again. I thought I should be tougher, but I just couldn't help it.

Section 5

The Investigation Begins

One of the hardest parts of the whole prosecution process was all the waiting. Especially waiting and not knowing what was going to happen to me, to Bob, to the other kids, and to my mom and dad.

Fortunately, at the beginning, I didn't have to wait very long before the **investigation** started happening. It was only three days later, although it seemed like ages, when Patrick O'Neill, my DSS social worker, called me at home. I was very nervous. He was very nice. He said I could call him "Pat."

First thing, Pat asked me how I was doing.

"OK."

Then he asked me if I understood why he was calling me. I knew all right, but it was a hard question to answer. He repeated the question, "Joe, do you know why I'm calling you this afternoon?"

"Because of Bob," I whispered into the phone. "Because I told Mr. Stone that Bob had sex with me."

"Yes," Pat said. Then he explained his role as my DSS social worker and the procedures.

In the middle of his explanation, I just blurted out this question that had been haunting my mind . . . for years probably. "Why did Bob do this to me?"

Patrick O'Neill was quiet for a minute, then he said, "I know this isn't a very good answer, Joe, but it's the only true answer I know." He took a very deep breath, kind of like a sigh, and continued. "The truth is, I don't know why Bob did these things to you. But I do know you did the right thing by telling us. So now we can stop Bob and help you. But Bob really needs help, too, so he doesn't hurt you or any other kids ever again."

I nodded in response, but of course Pat could not see my nod over the phone.

"Joe? Joe, are you still there?"

"Yeah, I'm here. I just don't understand."

"I'm really sorry I can't give you a better answer right now, Joe. But maybe as we get to know more about Bob we'll all understand this better."

"Yeah, yeah sure," I said. "It's OK."

Then Pat started to talk about this **team interview,** which he wanted to schedule as soon as possible. To him, soon meant within the next day or two. He said it was an important part of the DSS investigation, and it's done as a "team" so I won't have to be interviewed too many times by too many different people. He said, "We use the team interview here because we think it makes things easier for you and is better for the investigation. But in other places they do the interviewing differently, because they think other ways are easier for kids."

Pat went on to explain that they gather all the people who need to know what happened. That's my investigative social worker, Patrick O'Neill, the **assistant district attorney,** the **victim witness advocate,** the **child interview specialist,** a police officer, and a **therapist** from a local mental health clinic.

I almost had a heart attack on the spot when I realized I would have to say what Bob did in front of all those people, but Pat calmed me down right away. He said that I would only have to tell one person at the interview, and that would be the child interview specialist. The others would observe the interview from behind a two-way mirror. They would be able to see me and hear me, but I wouldn't be able to see or hear them. Telling one person sounded better, but I still didn't like the idea of more people knowing. It was embarrassing enough already, and the more people who knew, the more embarrassed I felt. I mean really, what was going to happen when the kids at school found out? I was really afraid and ashamed, I felt like I was shrinking. I was glad about that actually. I kept hoping that maybe I would totally disappear.

But Pat said if we were going to stop this type of abuse from happening to other kids, the people from the different agencies needed to know what happened to me. And, that meant that we needed to do the team interview. It was kind of cool that he said, "WE." I didn't feel so alone.

I knew that Pat and I needed to talk this over with Mom and Dad, but I also knew that my parents wanted Bob to be prosecuted. So, I knew the team interview would be happening. It was just a matter of time . . . a short time.

Section 6

The Interview

About 5:30 that same afternoon, Patrick O'Neill called back. He had called Dad at work and he wanted to let me know about the team interview. It was scheduled for 3:00 the next afternoon at the district attorney's office. They have a special Child Unit set up there to handle all the child abuse cases in the county.

Dad went with me to the **interview.** We arrived about ten minutes early. Pat was there and it was comforting to see him there. I felt a little bit better with him around because he had been so nice to me already. But I really couldn't get over how scary this was, and how exciting it was at the same time. I was amazed. All these important people, and my dad, were here because of me.

Everyone on the team was already meeting in a big conference room with a very long table and lots of chairs. At 3:00 p.m. this woman, Lisa, came out to the reception area where Dad and I were waiting. She was my interviewer. When she shook my hand, I did manage to glance up at her face. I was surprised to see that she looked very friendly. She said, "Hi, Joe. I'm Lisa Lance-White."

I mumbled, "Hello."

She smiled at me, and said, "I'll be conducting the interview with you today."

I mumbled again, "OK."

After another few minutes, Lisa and I went into a small, very neat room. In the room were two chairs, a small table, sort of like a coffee table, this huge mirror that covered one whole wall, and a box of tissues. It was weird, you know, sort of uncomfortable, to see myself in the mirror. I felt totally self-conscious. Lisa explained that the people on the team were on the other side of the mirror, and they could see and hear us. She said she thought it might be easier for me to talk with only her in the room. I knew it wasn't going to be easy for me, it didn't matter who was there.

Before the interview started, Lisa explained why certain people needed to observe. Pat would be observing as a part of his investigation for DSS. In his report, Pat needed to indicate whether or not he **supported the allegations** of the sexual abuse. The assistant district attorney would be making **prosecution** decisions, and the victim witness advocate would be concerned about how I'm feeling and reacting to all of this. I wasn't sure what it all meant, but I was sure this interview was important. As hard as it was for me to talk about Bob and the sexual abuse, I had to tell the truth. I had been dreaming about Bob . . . about those little guys in the van. Bob had to stop.

Then Lisa started asking questions. I was nervous. I couldn't focus my thoughts very well. I felt sick. I felt weird. I felt like crying. For awhile I didn't think I could breathe. Lisa asked me if I could speak louder. And then she asked me to tell exactly what Bob did. I didn't say it all. I could never say it all. But I made myself say some of it. Saying the words "penis" and "anus," talking about Bob and me and the other guys in the neighborhood club, made me feel ashamed and guilty. I know I mumbled. I'm very sure I stared at the floor most of the time, and shuffled my feet around a lot. I noticed some smudges on my new sneakers and a piece of string on the floor. Lisa had on black shoes. I remember. And then I didn't even realize it, but I started to cry. I covered my eyes because I didn't want anyone to know. Lisa noticed and she told me it was definitely OK to cry, but I tried not to.

Lisa was very understanding about me being so upset and nervous. She told me I was brave. I looked at her then, really confused, because I didn't feel anything resembling "brave" at that moment. But later I realized that buried somewhere deep underneath my confusion and upset, I felt proud of myself for being strong enough to do something to stop Bob.

After the interview, Lisa explained what would happen next. She said that if Dad and I wanted to talk with the team today, we could wait in the reception area while they reviewed my interview. We could meet with them today or later, separately or together. There was "no pressure," she said. It was totally my choice. I talked it over with Dad, and we decided to stay and meet my team.

Section 7

After the Interview

I wandered around the reception area for about twenty minutes while Dad tried to look calm and read a magazine he had taken out of his briefcase. I felt best about meeting with the team with Dad in the room, so when Lisa came out to get me, Dad and I went into the big conference room together. It was hard to be with all these people because I felt ashamed that they knew such private things about me. It was a struggle to even look at them, but when I did, I was surprised to see kind faces.

All the people in the room explained their job responsibilities to me, and what they would do next regarding my case. It was hard for me to understand everything they said. But it was mostly hard for me to even listen because I was so distracted by my own upset and embarrassment. But everyone was nice and patient. It was clear they were used to working with kids and that they knew what they were doing. I got the feeling that they were all on my side.

Patrick O'Neill spoke first. He said there was enough evidence to support the allegations of child sexual abuse in his report for DSS. Then the Assistant District Attorney, Nina Santiago, talked about the prosecution process. She explained that with my testimony, there appeared to be enough evidence to proceed with the criminal prosecution of Bob. She said the Commonwealth of Massachusetts would file the charges against him in **superior court.** She was careful to explain that I would not be responsible for taking Bob to court because the commonwealth is responsible for prosecuting people who commit crimes. But in order for the case to go forward, I needed to be willing to be a **witness.** My next interview would be videotaped and presented to the **grand jury.** Nina said my testimony would be taped so I would not have to say what happened live, in person, in front of the members of the grand jury.

I asked her what a grand jury was.

She said it was a jury of citizens who consider evidence brought before the superior court and decide if there is cause to believe a crime has been committed.

I told her I'd never heard of a "grand jury."

And so Nina explained more about it. She said that not all states have grand juries, and in those states, the **probable cause hearing** takes place before a judge. She also said that sometimes the states that do have grand juries don't use them for child abuse cases. "It is one of those legal procedures that really varies from state to state," she said. "And since we do have the grand jury here, we must present the evidence for your case to them. The videotaping of your **testimony** will hopefully make that part of the process easier for you, Joe. But, if the case goes to trial, you need to be able and willing to **testify** in court."

This information and my emotions were overwhelming. Although my team was very nice, they were also very serious about wanting Bob to take responsibility for what he did. I asked what would happen to Bob if the case went forward. My victim witness advocate, Andrew Kane, explained that there were a variety of possible **dispositions** of a criminal case, and that he and Nina would seek my input about what I would like to see happen if Bob were found **guilty**.

While Andrew was talking, I couldn't keep my eyes off of the police officer, Detective Rapucci. I wasn't planning to say anything, but I just blurted out the question anyway. "Are you going to arrest Bob?" I was upset about the possibility of Bob going to jail, and at the same time, that's exactly what I wanted to happen to him.

Detective Rapucci said he would not be arresting Bob at this time. He said he might ask Bob some questions, and would probably seek a warrant to search Bob's house for photographs and additional evidence, but would discuss everything with the assistant district attorney before deciding whether an arrest should be made.

Andrew continued the discussion by saying there would be time to talk about what might happen to Bob, and that my feelings would certainly be considered.

The next person to speak was the therapist from the mental health clinic. She said it was clear that this experience was upsetting for me, and assured me that upset was a normal reaction under the circumstances. I was relieved to be "normal." But then I started to cry when the therapist suggested that it might be helpful for me to talk with a counselor who works with kids my age. I was confused. A second ago I was "normal," and now I felt like there was something wrong with me because they wanted me to go to a **counselor.** I wondered if maybe these people thought I was crazy. I asked, kind of angry about it, and they all said they didn't think I was crazy. Patrick reminded me how important it would be for me to talk about my feelings and fears with someone I trusted.

Then Dad spoke for the first time. He said, "Joe's mother and I have already been looking into therapy for Joe, for all of us actually. We think it's important for Joe to have as much support through this process as we can provide for him."

I just looked at Dad, totally surprised. I didn't think that my parents believed too much in therapy. But everyone said they were pleased to hear there would be additional support in my life during this difficult time.

I wasn't sure how I felt about it, and I asked, "What if I don't want to go to a counselor?"

Dad said that I could think about it, and that I didn't have to do anything I didn't want to do.

"OK." That made me feel better about it. It felt important for me to be able to decide.

Dad asked the team if he and I could have a few minutes alone together to talk things over, so everyone left the room. Although a public trial would for sure be a hard experience for me, Dad and I decided that going forward with prosecution was the right thing to do. I'm telling you, I just could not get the picture of those little guys getting into Bob's van out of my mind. I wanted to make sure that he was stopped from hurting any more boys. Only God knew how many boys Bob had already abused. Dad agreed. We needed to stop Bob. But Dad also wanted me to know that his first priority was to help me. "Whatever you want to do, Joe."

I got a little teary when Dad said that, but I looked away because I didn't want him to know. I said I wanted to stop Bob.

When the team returned, Dad told them that we would cooperate with the district attorney's office in preparing the case against Bob for trial. They were all very businesslike as one by one, they thanked us.

Before we left the office, Andrew scheduled an appointment for me to come back to videotape the interview of my testimony for the grand jury. Then he said, "The police will begin an investigation, and they might be in contact with some of the other guys from the Neighborhood Club."

I just nodded, wondering again what I had done.

Andrew gave me his business card, and told me I could call him if I had any questions about the legal process, or didn't understand something that happened, or even if I just wanted to talk to somebody. I put his card in my backpack along with Pat's. Having their telephone numbers with me all the time helped me feel safe somehow.

As Dad and I were leaving the office, Andrew shook our hands and said he would be in touch very soon. He said it was his job to answer my questions, explain the court process, provide support to me and my family, and keep me notified of the case status. He also said that he had originally hoped to explain the court process to me that afternoon, but it seemed like too much for one day. "Another time, then, OK?" he asked.

That was fine with me.

Andrew looked right at me, and assured me he would be there for me. And I believed him.

Section 8

Counseling

I went to school the next couple days, and being there was a relief. I wanted to forget all about Bob and abuse and going to court. I wanted to pretend that everything was just fine with me.

I hadn't told any of my friends or teachers what was going on. But I knew I needed to talk to some of the other guys who were at Bob's with me. And I knew I needed to talk to them soon. I just didn't know what to say. I wanted them to agree with my decision to testify against Bob. But what if they didn't? What if they protected Bob and said I lied? After all, we all took an oath never to tell.

I didn't know what to do. I was afraid if I told even one friend that all the other kids would find out and then they would tease me. They might think it was all my fault, or that I wanted Bob to have sex with me. I didn't think I was overreacting, because I know how mean kids can be to each other. They can get ahold of any piece of information and torment a guy to death with it. I've seen it. I know. Every time I started to imagine what they were going to say about me, or what they were going to do to me, I shuddered. I felt afraid and ashamed.

My parents convinced me that seeing a therapist was a good idea. I guess I did need to talk to someone. I went to see Dr. Catherine Clayton. She said I could call her "Cathy." I liked that better than calling her "Doctor."

During that first appointment, I couldn't talk much about anything. I stared out the window, and at the floor. I fidgeted. I didn't want to look at Cathy at all. She didn't say anything about my nervous behavior, and when the time was up I scheduled another appointment for two days later. I didn't know how this was going to help me, especially if I couldn't or didn't talk about anything, but having the appointment made me feel better.

When I was leaving the office, Cathy gave me her business card with her telephone number on it. She told me I could call her any time, day or night, if I wanted to talk to her . . . or if I wanted her to talk to me. I smiled, I actually smiled, when I put Cathy's card into my backpack with Patrick's and Andrew's. I felt like I had a whole team of people in there helping me get through this.

During my next appointment with Cathy, I was calmer. I had made a list of things I wanted to talk about. My questions were written on a piece of paper that was folded about thirty times and stuffed into the inside pocket of my jacket.

First on my list was what to do about feeling so isolated. I still hadn't told anyone. Although I didn't want to feel so alone, I also didn't want anyone else to know. But I knew it wasn't going to be a secret for long. I mean, there were a lot of other guys at Bob's. I saw him abusing them, just like he did to me. I knew I needed to deal with this before the police talked to the other kids. But maybe they already talked to them, and the other guys were feeling the same worries as me about talking to anyone else. This situation seemed liked a volcano getting ready to explode, and I wanted to be braced for it.

Second on my list was my mixed emotions about what I called my "sexual identity." It was confusing to me because I liked being around girls, but lots of times the sexual experiences with Bob felt really good. I didn't know what it meant, but I wondered if it meant that I was gay.

And then I started to worry about "practical" things. Like what if Bob had AIDS, or some other sexually transmitted disease. When I thought about AIDS, I started to panic, so I tried not to think about it.

I was so ashamed about all of this that sometimes I wanted to hide out, or be invisible maybe. I figured people could tell that I'd had all those sexual experiences for all those years just by looking at me. I felt ruined.

I still couldn't figure out why Bob did this to me, and to all the other kids. I asked Cathy "Why?" over and over. It was too hard for me to understand. I kept wishing it didn't happen.

Finally I managed to tell Cathy that I had been feeling so terrible and nervous when I was alone at night that I actually thought I might rather be dead than to feel this way. I thought maybe she would be surprised by this because I had been trying to hide my real feelings, and thought I was being "totally cool" about it all. But I wasn't feeling all that cool. I was having these horrible nightmares. I also wasn't sure if I did the right thing by telling, or if I was doing the right thing by planning to testify. I felt guilty. Bob might go to jail, and maybe it wasn't his fault. I mean he didn't force me. I liked what we did. I liked how it made me feel. It was hard for me to admit, but sometimes I wanted him to do it. Lots of times I even called him to get together.

I told Cathy I wasn't sure if I felt like swearing or crying. She said it was fine to go ahead and do either or both, but I was too embarrassed.

Cathy sat quietly while I went down my list of questions and concerns, which I read pretty fast, stumbling over a lot of my scribbled words. When I finally finished, I looked up at her over the crumpled piece of paper I held in my hands, and she smiled at me. Then she leaned forward a little bit and she said, "Joe, I can see that you are feeling nervous and sad and confused about all of this. And before I say anything else, I want to tell you that it is completely normal under these circumstances to be experiencing all of those feelings."

What a relief! I breathed, I think, for the first time since I came into her office that day. I felt myself relax a little.

Cathy continued. "Your list is terrific, Joe. I can see that you worked very hard putting it together, and I know it took a lot of strength to put your thoughts and feelings onto paper and bring them here."

Then she said that dealing with sexual abuse issues was tough for everyone, and that it was "a real act of courage" for me to tell Mr. Stone about Bob.

Cathy also said she was glad I trusted her enough to bring my list to her. She said we would talk about whatever I wanted whenever I wanted, whether it was on the list or not. "We can talk about the details of the abuse when you feel ready to do that, Joe. That will be an important part of our work together. But it's also important for us to talk about your reactions to what is happening in your life right now regarding the trial, as well as your relationships with your family and your friends, and the experiences you are having at school." It felt good not to be pressured to talk about what Bob did right then.

Unfortunately, Cathy didn't think we'd be able to answer all of my questions in that hour on that day. I was upset about this because I really wanted the answers. But she asked me to say where I wanted to begin, and we would begin. And so we did. It was hard to talk about my feelings. My fear about doing this was huge. But I made myself do it as best as I could. Somewhere deep down inside, I knew it was important to get my feelings out of me and into the world. Cathy helped me to talk by asking me clear and direct questions.

The hour passed quickly, but it was a hard time for me. We decided I would come to see her on Mondays and Thursdays for the next month. That way, Cathy said, I wouldn't feel so isolated and alone.

Because I didn't talk about it, and because Cathy knew that wanting to be dead rather than deal with all of this on my list, she said she wanted to take some extra time before I left to talk a bit about those feelings, if that was OK with me.

"That's OK," I said, but I couldn't look at her. I was too ashamed.

Cathy suggested that I keep the telephone number of the twenty-four-hour crisis line Ms. Feldman gave me handy at all times. She encouraged me to use it, to talk to someone there, especially another teenager, if I wanted. She reminded me that everything I said would be kept absolutely private. Cathy asked me to promise that the next time I felt so bad, I would call her, no matter what time.

"Yeah, OK," I promised, but I knew I wouldn't. I didn't want to bother her.

I couldn't believed what she said then. "Honestly, Joe, anytime will be fine to call. You won't be bothering me at all. If I'm tied up when you call, I'll get back to you just as soon as I can."

I nodded, but inside I thought, "She read my mind."

Cathy suggested that I put the crisis line telephone number and her telephone number on a piece of paper right next to my bed so they would be there for me at night when I was feeling scared and alone.

Section 9

Prosecution Begins

The next week, my victim witness advocate, Andrew Kane—he said everyone called him Drew and that I could, too, if I wanted—called from the district attorney's office. He wanted to follow up on our meeting and to answer any questions I might have. He also wanted to explain the investigation, interview, and court processes to me.

But before doing any of that, Drew asked me how I was feeling. He asked about my therapy, "How's that counseling going?"

"OK."

Drew said that he knew this was really hard for me. He assured me that the case would only be brought to trial if my therapist, my parents and I thought it was advisable for me. Everyone wanted to make sure I would be OK, and that the court process was the right choice for me.

We confirmed a date for making a videotape to present to the grand jury. Then Drew offered me some options for talking about the details of the prosecution process. He said we could talk on the phone, or meet earlier on the day of the interview, or I could come into the office for a separate meeting. I decided I wanted to come in to his office to see him, so we scheduled a meeting for the next day after school.

When we got together the next afternoon, Drew explained more about the grand jury. He said, "The grand jury consists of a group of citizens who are registered to vote in our county. They are called for jury duty and are assigned to review the evidence for superior court cases for about three months. Their job is to hear evidence on serious cases to determine if the case should go forward into the superior court system."

He continued, "Nina will present the case against Bob to the grand jury, and then the jury will watch the videotape of your testimony. Neither Bob nor his lawyer will be here. And because your testimony is on tape, you don't have to be there either. After the grand jury reviews the evidence, they vote on whether or not they think there is sufficient evidence to prosecute. If they think YES, they issue an **indictment.** If they think NO, this case is closed."

All these legal terms sounded like a foreign language to me, and I was pretty confused. So confused actually, that I didn't know what to ask when Drew wanted to know if I had any questions.

He went on to explain about the **criminal justice system.** He said it was designed to protect the rights of the accused, which was Bob. He was accused of sexually abusing me. Drew reminded me of the phrase we learned in junior high civics class, **"presumed innocent** until proven guilty." The assistant district attorney had to convince a trial **jury,** beyond a **reasonable doubt,** that Bob was guilty of abusing me.

Drew told me that the criminal court system is designed for adults and that it sometimes can be especially hard for kids. "Things can be said, things can happen," he said, "that kids don't understand. But I'm always here to help you, Joe. Please, just ask me. Anything. Feel free to ask me anything."

Finally I did manage to ask a few questions, just to see if I could make some sense of all that Drew was saying. Then I realized it would be helpful to write some things down in case I forgot, or so I could think about this and ask more questions later.

Before we ended the conversation, Drew reminded me again that it was OK for me to call him if I wanted to talk about the case or if I had any questions. I'm not really the type to ask a lot of questions or to call people, but it seemed that so far everyone—Pat, Cathy, Drew— kept inviting me, encouraging me to call whenever, and to ask whatever. I began to think that maybe I wouldn't be such a bother after all.

Drew reminded me again of my appointment with Lisa to videotape the Grand Jury interview. He also reminded me that it would only happen if I felt ready. He assured me I could decide if and when the time was right for the interview. Drew and Nina, the **ADA,** would be there observing the interview from behind the two-way mirror.

Drew said he would call my parents some time during the next few days to tell them what happens next and to answer their questions.

"Good-bye, Joe." Drew said as he walked me to the door of the office. "Take care. And call me. I'm here for you."

I felt some tears in my eyes. "Bye, Drew. And thanks," I said.

I stood outside the building for a long time, staring at the cars whizzing by. Everyone seemed to be going somewhere. That's where I wanted to go. Somewhere. Anywhere away from here. I suddenly felt furious that this was happening to me. Why? Why did I have to deal with this?

Section 10

Pretrial Testimony

My mom went with me to the district attorney's office on the day we were making the videotape for the grand jury. These past few weeks had been a really hard time for my family. Mom and Dad had also been to see a therapist, and I felt guilty about that. I mean, if I had just kept quiet about Bob, everything would be just like it had been a month ago. Fine. Everything would be just fine. Cathy told me over and over that none of this was my fault, and that Mom and Dad going to a therapist was a good thing. It showed that they were committed to helping me. I was confused. Cathy helped me sort things out when I was confused.

Lisa, Drew, and Nina Santiago were all going to be a part of the interviewing process. Before beginning the taping, they spent some time just talking to me. Although I felt nervous beneath my "totally cool" act, I also felt like a very important person at a business meeting with other important people. I tried to act especially cool because I didn't want anyone to know I was really "totally nervous."

Drew asked me how I was feeling.

I said, "Fine."

He asked how my therapy was going and how I liked Cathy.

"Fine. Fine."

Drew wanted to make sure I would be OK if I gave my testimony that day, and when I told him I was ready, and would be seeing Cathy later, he said that was a "good plan." It was Cathy's idea for me to see her after the interview. That way I would feel "supported," she said.

The interview room was the same room I was in before when I talked to Lisa. Everything was just the same. I sat in a chair facing the mirror and the camera hiding behind it. Lisa spoke to the mirror and asked for the camera to be turned on. Drew and Nina were behind the mirror, so I guess one of them did it.

Lisa spoke to the camera. "Good afternoon. Today is December 8. My name is Lisa Lance-White from the district attorney's office. I'm here today meeting with Joe."

Then Lisa spoke to me. "Joe, do you understand that it is important for you to tell the truth when you answer the questions I'm going to ask you today?"

I answered, "Yes," but my voice was very soft because there was a huge lump in my throat, and Lisa asked me to speak louder. I said it again, "YES."

Then she asked, "Do you promise to tell the truth today, Joe?"

I replied, "Yes, I do." I felt a shiver go through my body. I shut my eyes tight and took a deep breath. I was really doing this!

Lisa began asking me some simple questions like my full name, my birthday, where I went to school, what grade I was in, my address, and Bob's address. While I was answering those questions, Lisa had to remind me a couple of times to speak up.

I was very nervous, and even laughed a couple of times during those first questions. I couldn't believe I laughed because it definitely was not a funny experience, but I was just so nervous and scared. I laughed, I think, to keep from crying. I actually clutched the arms of my chair the whole time, maybe so I wouldn't get up and run away.

And then came the hard questions. Lisa asked, "Joe, did something happen with your neighbor Bob? What happened? When did it begin? How often did it happen? Where did it happen? Who was there? When did it stop? . . ." As I answered these questions for Lisa, I remember reaching up and touching my face. It felt so hot.

It seemed like I was in the interview room answering these questions forever. I was surprised to find out that the whole thing only took about fifteen minutes.

At the end of the interview Lisa thanked me, and we went back out into the reception area to get Mom. Then we all met for a short time in the big conference room. Nina, Drew, and Lisa said that my testimony was "excellent." But all I cared about was that it was over. I just knew I did the right thing, and I felt so relieved.

Drew said he would call in a couple of days to discuss the next step. That's what I liked best about Drew, he kept me informed and he always called me when he said he would. That was so important because I really needed someone to count on.

When we left the office, Mom offered to take me to McDonald's, but I wasn't hungry. Later I went to see Cathy.

Section 11

Counseling Support

Have I mentioned how tired I was? During those weeks after I first told Mr. Stone about Bob, I was so tired all the time. Sometimes I felt sick and I didn't eat much. I was also very confused. Yes, for sure. I felt tired and sick and confused that afternoon when I went to see Cathy.

I know it's hard for people to understand, but I loved Bob, and I felt guilty about turning him in. And now my testimony was on video-tape. A grand jury was going to hear what Bob did to me. I was embarrassed even thinking about it. I was also sad because I didn't want Bob to get into any trouble, and I didn't want Bob to be mad at me. When I saw Cathy I told her I wasn't sure that I should be involved in the prosecution process.

Cathy said she understood my confusion. That afternoon she helped me to understand it too, and to accept being confused. I wanted everything in my life to be fine and smooth and simple, and for everyone I knew, including Bob, to be happy. I felt like such a troublemaker.

Cathy said it was OK for me to love Bob and to still want him to take responsibility for his actions. After all, Bob abused me. "Bob has some problems, Joe, and he needs help," Cathy said. "However," she continued, "what he did was also a crime. Legally it was wrong, and morally it was wrong." She explained that the child abuse laws were made to protect me, and that I, and all those other "little guys" I kept mentioning, had a right to be protected. Cathy and everyone at the district attorney's office had a way of making me feel important. Since they believed that I had "rights," I came to believe it, too.

Pat O'Neill told me, and Lisa told me and Drew told me that if testifying felt too hard for me, I could withdraw from the process and stop the prosecution at any time. Although other guys might come forward and be willing to testify, for the time being, I was the primary witness. Without my cooperation, there was really no case.

Cathy reminded me again that feeling reluctant about the court process is normal. Then she said, "Know that you do have a choice about testifying, Joe."

I left Cathy's office feeling less tired, but I was definitely lost in thought about what she told me. I was "important." I had "rights." I could "choose." I felt better because I knew I had some control over my life.

Section 12

Waiting

The holiday season came and went. I hardly noticed. However, I did notice that those weeks after my interview seemed endless. I think the time seemed longer than it really was because I didn't know what was happening. And mostly it didn't seem that anything was happening. But, even though I couldn't tell, the justice system was, in fact, operating.

Some of the time I was kind of in a panic, and I think I called either Drew or Nina or both of them at least once a day to see how my case was going. I needed to know. Nina was in court a lot, so sometimes she couldn't call me back right away and I would panic even more, worrying that she forgot me. But Drew always called me, and even though he sometimes didn't have much new information, just talking to him helped me to calm down.

Then finally, one day after school, Drew called. *The Commonwealth of Massachusetts vs. Bob* would be heard by the grand jury the following Tuesday. "And then shortly after that," he said, "we'll know if an indictment will be issued." I felt a surge of excitement rush through my body that shot like an electric current up and down my back and through my legs and arms.

But when I hung up the phone I went numb. I sat in the living room for a long time waiting for my parents to come home from work. As the sun went down I watched the house get dark, and the shadows appear. I never even turned on the lights. I wasn't even sure if I could move. The only sound I noticed was the ticking of the clock.

Waiting . . . waiting . . . it seemed like forever.

Section 13

At School

Some days it was great to go to school. The distraction of school was good. But some days I didn't want to go. Sometimes it felt best to put on my earphones, turn up the music—loud—and just walk. It didn't matter where to. I felt lost in the music, and safe wandering around. I was sure that Bob was following me to school. I was afraid of him.

My mom had a meeting with the principal at school, who then talked with all of my teachers. Without being specific, the principal explained that I was experiencing a " personal crisis," and that I might be late or absent, and that sometimes I might have difficulty concentrating, or that maybe I would need some extra help with my work or some extra attention. I was embarrassed about getting any special treatment because I didn't want the other kids to notice it and give me a hard time. But deep down, I appreciated everyone's help and concern. And this truly was a crisis.

Cathy and Mom helped me decide which friends to tell and how to tell them. Cathy also helped prepare me for their possible reactions, especially the other guys who I knew Bob had also abused. It was going to be totally hard if they denied it happened to them, or especially if they denied it happened to me.

My parents really helped with this. They talked to my friends' parents so they could understand what was happening, and to offer them support if their sons had also been involved. It felt weird to me when this secret thing wasn't a secret anymore. I felt ashamed, but I needed people to know so I could feel supported, so they could help me deal with all of this.

I sometimes felt as if the whole world knew my dirty secret. I just knew that everyone was looking at me. I wished that no one could see me. I prayed that one day I would disappear and then it would all be over.

Even on the days I felt like going to school I didn't say much in classes because I didn't want to attract attention. I didn't know what to say to people, even my friends. Should I talk about what was constantly nagging at my thoughts—Bob and the trial? Should I bring it up to the other guys I knew were involved? Or, should I talk about sports and music and classes and dates, and just pretend that everything was cool? It was hard. I didn't know what to do, how to be, where to start.

It helped a lot when my friends would come up to me and start conversations. Like at lunch one day, Dan came over and said, "Hey, Joe. So what do you think about that substitute teacher in history class? Is he a total bore or what?" He broke the ice, and just acted natural around me. I remember smiling that day. I didn't feel so isolated or weird.

I was pretty nervous and jumpy a lot. One day at school the hall was kind of empty and I was getting a notebook from my locker. This girl, Joy, called to me from down the hall. "Hi, Joe!" She startled me and I dropped all of my books from my locker on my foot. I felt so stupid. Joy helped me pick up my stuff. She said she was sorry for startling me. I was embarrassed. But whatever it was she said next started me laughing. It felt good to laugh!

That afternoon after school, Joy and Dan and I went out for some fries and a Coke. I had fun. We didn't talk about my real life. The trial, I mean. We talked about school and movies and concerts. It was so good just to have some fun.

As things about the abuse and the trial became public, more people found out. And not all the kids were as nice to me as Joy and Dan. Some were cruel, and I hated them. Some days I thought I'd never go back to school. Some days I was going to leave town, change my name, and start a whole new life. Cathy helped me through the tears and hate about those kids. It's times of trouble like this that you find out who your true friends are.

I was beginning to learn about trust. I had been pretty mixed up about that.

Section 14

The Indictment

It had been an uneventful day. I was beginning to feel a little calmer, and didn't even jump when the phone rang at home late that afternoon. It was Drew calling to tell me that the grand jury had handed down an indictment against Bob. He said that because Bob still had access to kids, a **warrant** had been issued and Bob would be arrested. The **arraignment** would be in superior court within the next few days. My hand felt frozen to the phone. Bob going to jail. My thoughts were whirling.

I knew that Drew had explained arraignment to me before, but I guess I forgot. I wanted to understand, so I asked him, "What's arraignment, again?"

He explained. "Arraignment is the public reading in court of the formal charges against Bob. At this time, the charges filed against Bob will be read to him, and he will **plead** 'guilty' or 'not guilty.' Just so you know, Joe, it is pretty standard for all defendants charged with serious crimes to plead "not guilty" at the time of arraignment. This has nothing to do with whether or not they plead guilty later in the process. Joe? Joe, are you still there?"

I was there, but I had drifted off into my whirling thoughts. Was this all really happening? I came back, "Yeah, yeah."

"Oh, by the way, Joe," Drew continued, "remember we mentioned that although it's not very common, sometimes indictments handed down by the grand jury might appear in the local newspapers. It's more likely in this case to get news coverage because of the number of potential victims, but your name won't be revealed. The law in the commonwealth says the media cannot use your name. However, Bob's name and address might be in the papers."

"Oh no," I said. "Now everyone will know." I hid my face in my hands and just cried. Drew said that he understood I was upset and frightened about being publicly exposed. He spent a lot of time that afternoon talking with me, listening to me . . . comforting and supporting me.

Section 15

The Arraignment

Generally, time was moving very slowly for me. But the day of the arraignment arrived quickly. I didn't have to go to the arraignment. It was a "brief procedure," Nina said, so she was the only one who needed to be there. She said it was important for Bob to understand that the charges were being brought against him by the Common-wealth of Massachusetts, not by me or any of the other boys who might be witnesses. That fact would be clearer to Bob if I wasn't there for the arraignment. But I might as well have been there, though, be-cause I couldn't think of anything else all day. I imagined the scene over and over in my mind. I could see the court officers leading Bob into the room. Would he be handcuffed? That image troubled me. Bob, handcuffed. All because of me.

Late in the day Drew called. I stayed home from school waiting to hear form him. Believe me, it was a very long day! As expected, Bob pled "not guilty." They had a **bail hearing,** and **bail** was set so Bob wouldn't have to be in jail before the trial. I was nervous about that. I worried that Bob would come after me to get even with me for telling.

Awhile ago, I told Nina I was worried that Bob was following me to school, and she got a **restraining order,** "to keep you safe," she said. But I was really worried now. Bob indicted and out on bail. Drew interrupted my worries by saying that court dates had been set for a **pretrial conference** and **motions hearing.** But I didn't have to go to them. "The actual trial date," he said, "could be scheduled any-time from three months to a year from now."

"A year!" I yelled at him. I know I yelled even though I didn't mean to. "A year!" I was totally shocked.

Drew said calmly, "Joe, it might even be longer. Sometimes there are **continuances** in court which we can't control. Realistically the trial could happen in October or November." This was January. October, November. That seemed like never.

After I calmed down, I called Drew back. "What's a continuance?" I needed to hear the explanation again even though I knew Drew had explained this to me before. And so he explained it to me again. "A continuance is a change in the date when something is scheduled to happen in court."

Now I had more questions: "Why does that happen? Will it happen to me?"

He answered, "A continuance happens for a lot of different reasons. Sometimes the lawyers need to do more research on the legal issues. Sometimes a witness is not available. Sometimes a previously scheduled trial takes longer than expected, so the judge is busy with that and not ready for us." Drew didn't know if a continuance would happen for us. "But if it does," he said, "we will most likely be notified well in advance about any delays or changes. When it is time for the trial you will receive a **subpoena** telling you when to appear in court. By then, things should be pretty well set and ready to go."

Section 16

Waiting Again

I just could not believe that it took so long for a trial to be held in superior court. It's about "scheduling" they told me, and lots of cases for the judges to hear. It was hard for me because there was nothing I could do about it but wait. Sometimes I was very nervous inside because of all the waiting, and mostly there was just nothing anyone could do about it.

Eventually I settled down into a routine, and a routine felt nice for a change. I still called Drew a lot with questions and needing updates. He called me regularly to check in about how I was doing and to keep me informed about the progress of the case. I saw Cathy every week, and I started to feel OK about her, and to trust her, too. Sometimes I wasn't sure why I went to see Cathy because I didn't really want to talk about the abuse. Sometimes I just wanted to forget the whole thing.

Things were quiet at home. My parents said they wanted to help me, and they did by being there for me. We didn't talk about the trial or the abuse or Bob very much because Mom and Dad usually waited for me to bring it up, which wasn't often.

Mom would make attempts to talk about it by saying things like, "How are you feeling about 'things' today?" But since she was never too specific in her questions, I was never too specific in my answers either.

Usually I said something like, "Yeah, it's cool."

It was all so hard for me to talk about. But even though I didn't say much to my parents, I appreciated their love and support. They consistently asked me how I was doing. And even though they didn't say directly "about Bob and the trial," I knew what they meant. I knew they were there to help me. Eventually, with Cathy's help, I was able to tell my parents how I was, and to thank them for their support.

Section 17

The Empty Courtroom

Although I went on with my regular life, I felt as if a gray storm cloud was hovering over me all the time. It followed me everywhere. I wondered if Bob had one, too.

In mid-August, Drew called to tell me that a trial date had been set for October 4. I shivered, and it was 90 degrees outside! He reminded me, right then, that things could come up to cause delays.

In September, Nina, Drew, and I met a few times to go over what would happen in court. First they talked to me about the verdict. Drew said, "We know Bob is guilty, Joe. But during the trial, we need to prove his guilt, beyond a reasonable doubt. Remember? We talked about reasonable doubt."

I nodded.

Drew was being very serious. "In cases like this, sometimes the **defendant** is found **not guilty.** If that happens, Joe, it doesn't mean that Bob is innocent, or that he didn't abuse you. It means that the district attorney's office did not provide sufficient evidence to convince the jury of his guilt beyond a reasonable doubt." Drew told me that to prepare me for the possibility that Bob might be **acquitted** rather than **convicted.** I knew it was a possibility, but I told Drew that I didn't even want to think about it. I couldn't think about it.

One morning Drew and Nina took me to an empty courtroom so I wouldn't be going into a totally strange place when the trial started. We went into the courtroom. It looked dark and somber, and felt cold. In fact, a shiver went up my back as I stood in the doorway and looked around. I knew right away this was a serious place.

Nina coaxed me into sitting in the **witness stand.** She and Drew were going through some papers deciding on what questions to ask me. They were talking together, and I sat in the stand and looked around. I had to remind myself to breathe. I felt hot. Tears started welling up in my eyes. I squeezed my eyes shut really tight, hoping the tears would go away, hoping when I opened my eyes I would be away. In Florida maybe, in Hawaii, or maybe Spain. I've always wanted to go to Spain. My hands clutched the arms of the chair. I was hoping with all my might.

And then I heard Drew's voice. "Joe. Joe. What's happening?"

I opened my eyes and was surprised to see him and Nina and the empty courtroom. It didn't look so scary now because it wasn't the first time I was seeing it. It actually looked familiar.

"I'm OK," I said. So while I continued to sit in the stand, supposedly "getting comfortable," Nina spent some time preparing me for what might come up in the trial. This was going to be hard.

When I stepped down from the stand, I felt a little shaky, but I also felt very mature and grown-up.

Section 18

Pretrial Details

A lot of paperwork goes into a trial. I learned that first thing. Before the trial actually happens, the ADA and the **defense attorney** meet in court with the **judge** and the other court workers (the **court officers,** the **judge's clerk,** and the **court reporter**), to submit and decide about the **pretrial motions.** That's when the attorneys address certain legal issues with the judge, including special procedures and special conditions. For example, Nina asked for a microphone to use during my testimony. She knew I had a hard time speaking up when it came to the details of the abuse. She wanted to make sure the judge, the jury, and everyone could hear me. The defense attorney didn't want Nina to refer to me as a **victim,** but to use the term **complaining witness** instead. Drew explained that this was because the word victim implied that Bob hurt me and that is what the prosecution has to prove. It was a "technicality," he said.

The judge decided to "wait and see" about the microphone, but I wish he hadn't done that. He instructed Nina to use the phrase "complaining witness" instead of victim.

The court process—the whole thing—was really hard for me. Sometimes I didn't understand what was going on, and sometimes I really started to wonder whose side they were on.

Section 19

Delays and Preparations

There were continuances. I'm glad Nina and Drew warned me about them, but even their warnings didn't help my stress about all the delays. I'd be all ready for the trial to start, and either Drew or Nina would call to say it had to be rescheduled for later.

It happened a few times, and each time I got mad at Drew or Nina, whichever one called to tell me the news. But then I felt bad about being mad at them. They were really nice to me, and on my side, I knew it. After all, the judge was the person who was in charge of the courtroom, and the delays were mostly for "administrative reasons," they said. Nina and Drew assured me it was nothing personal against me. But I could never figure out how those reasons, whatever they were, could be more important than a person's feelings. I was very upset about all this waiting and delaying. I kept wondering if they cared about me at all. I had waited so long already, and I didn't know if I could stand waiting one minute longer. Dad called my upset "apprehension." Fear of future evil! That felt like an accurate description. But, somehow, I made it through all the waiting.

For months before the trial I spent some of my free time preparing myself by watching lawyer shows on television. I almost never missed *Judge Judy* or *Law and Order* or *The Practice*. And sometimes I'd stay up late and watch the old reruns of the original *Perry Mason*. I prayed that Nina was a better prosecutor than poor Mr. Burger!

The television law fascinated me. Even though Drew talked to me a lot about the legal process and the language that would be used in court, I thought I could become some kind of "expert" through my TV research. And then, I'd be less afraid. Drew and Nina both talked to me about television law, warning me that some of it was "realistic" and some of it was "just drama" geared to entertain TV audiences. But I watched the shows anyway.

Unfortunately, those TV shows didn't help me to feel more confident when my real day in court finally came. But they did keep me occupied during the long months of waiting. Watching them helped me feel that I was doing something productive to prepare myself.

Section 20

The Trial Begins

The trial was finally scheduled to begin on November 11. "A firm date," Nina said. I received a subpoena in the mail requesting my appearance as a witness for the prosecution in the case of *The Commonwealth of Massachusetts vs. Bob.* I was impressed by the official-looking importance of the document, so I hung it up on the wall in my room. It felt like a "Red Badge of Courage."

The trial did start on November 11. It lasted for five days from the jury **empaneling** to the reading of the **verdict.** Those were by far the longest, yet the shortest, five days of my entire life. When the trial was in progress, even the minutes crawled by. The days seemed endless. And the sleepless nights were definitely endless. But when the trial was all over, it seemed to have lasted no longer than the blink of an eye.

Section 21

In Court

Court was a tense place. It was extremely organized, and the people who worked there seemed to know exactly what was going on. But in spite of their knowing, even they seemed tense.

There were a lot of people in court. There were two lawyers (Nina and Mr. McCarthy, who was the defense attorney for Bob). There were two court officers. They had on uniforms sort of like police officers. There was a court clerk who sat at a desk in front of the judge's bench, and a court reporter who recorded every word of the trial. I was surprised that there were fourteen people on the jury instead of twelve. I kept counting them, thinking I made a mistake. When I asked Drew, he explained that two jurors were alternates in case someone on the jury got sick or something. There were also a few people in the audience. Drew explained that most trials are open to the public. I wanted to know who the people were and why they were there.

I appreciated Drew more as each minute passed. He stayed with me the whole time. I didn't realize it, but I couldn't be in the courtroom through the whole trial. There's this thing called being **sequestered.** It means that one witness can't hear the testimony of other witnesses, so as not to be influenced by what someone else says. So I had to spend a lot of time with Drew in the victim/witness "waiting" room (what a perfect name for it), wondering what in the world was going on inside the courtroom. There was this huge clock on the wall in the waiting room, and I just stared at it, watching the endless seconds tick by. At first I asked Drew a lot of questions because I was so nervous, but then I drifted off into my own thoughts. I was so worried. I was going to have to say all those embarrassing things in the courtroom. But I had to do it. I wanted Bob off the streets, away from helpless kids.

I was at the courthouse on the third, fourth, and fifth days of the trial. Mom and Dad were there with me the whole time. We didn't have to be there for the jury selection or the pretrial motions which happened during the first two days.

When the actual trial part started, Nina and Mr. McCarthy gave their **opening statements.** Then Nina called me to the witness stand to testify. My hands were sweaty. My stomach was upset. And for a minute I thought I might throw up, but I didn't. It was hard to testify, for sure. But I did it. I was OK.

Nina stood across the courtroom and asked me questions. The easy ones were first. My name, address, age, school, where I live . . . and then came the hard ones. Nina began to ask me questions about the sexual experiences I had with Bob. Oh no. She kept asking me to speak up, but I could barely speak at all.

Then, all of a sudden, the judge jumped up from his chair. This un-expected movement, right in the middle of my testimony, startled me. He abruptly said, "We're in **recess.** Counsel, in my chambers." Sur-rounded by a cloud of swirling black fabric, the judge disappeared from the courtroom, followed by the lawyers.

I started to cry. I couldn't help it. I couldn't figure out what was happening. But then, I was out in the corridor and Drew was right be-side me. I got some water, and Drew tried to comfort me. The next thing I knew, the court officers were installing a microphone on the witness stand for me to use. Nina came out into the corridor and ex-plained that the judge couldn't hear my answers and asked that the microphone be set up. I wished that the judge had approved Nina's pretrial motion for a microphone in the first place, because now I was upset and feeling afraid of him.

Fifteen minutes later court was back in session, I was back in the witness stand. The judge spoke to me directly and apologized for the disruption. He asked me to speak clearly into the microphone, "So the jury can hear every word." I think he smiled at me. I didn't smile back. I just nodded.

Section 22

Cross-Examination

When Nina finished asking me questions, Bob's lawyer, Mr. McCarthy, **cross-examined** me. He was loud and abrupt. At times I felt attacked by him. He tried to confuse me by asking me the same question over in different ways.

Mr. McCarthy's confusing questions were making it hard for me to think. I was getting really tense and I felt hot tears stinging my eyes. My fists were clenched in my lap. I wanted to run out of the courtroom, and not stop running until I got to Spain. But I tried to hold it together, and I answered the questions in the best way I could. Mr. McCarthy kept saying he didn't understand. So he'd ask the same question again, and again. I didn't know what to do. Finally, the judge interrupted. He clearly rephrased Mr. McCarthy's last question, which had been asked several times, and my answer. He then looked directly at me and asked, "Is this what you're saying, Joe?"

"Yes," I said as I nodded.

The judge turned to Bob's lawyer and said, "Well, then. That's quite enough for this question, Mr. McCarthy. I think that both the jury and I understand the witness's answer. Please move on."

I felt such relief, I can't even say. The judge's interruption helped me to calm down, and Mr. McCarthy didn't seem so mean from then on. But still, I was totally glad when it was finally over. I was questioned for almost three hours.

That afternoon and part of the next day there were other witnesses. After that, Bob testified even though his lawyer didn't want him to, and he didn't have to. Drew explained that Bob didn't have to testify because of the **Fifth Amendment,** and because the **burden of proof** is on the prosecution. A couple of people testified for Bob as **character witnesses.** I didn't hear any of the testimony because I was sequestered.

At the end of the examination of all of the witnesses, both lawyers gave their **closing arguments** to the court, first the defense attorney, Mr. McCarthy, and then Nina. I was there for that. It was very scary hearing Mr. McCarthy speak. He seemed so convinced that Bob was not guilty. He said that I was mistaken. "Children misunderstand and misinterpret." He said that I lied. "Children have vivid imaginations, and they sometimes fabricate dramatic tales to get attention." That's what Mr. McCarthy had to say about me. Drew had prepared me for the types of things Mr. McCarthy might say, but it was still hard for me not to get angry and scared.

But Nina's closing argument restored my faith and confidence. She said, "Why would Joe lie? Why would he come before this court and this jury and discuss the most embarrassing, painful details of his life? Being here, talking about sexual abuse is absolutely the last thing a teenaged boy wants to do. Joe has no reason to lie."

I felt like I was on a roller coaster. I wondered how the jury felt.

Section 23

Instructions to the Jury

After the closing arguments, the judge spoke directly the jury for what seemed to be a very long time. I wondered how they could remember everything he said.

The judge told the jury to weigh the **credibility** of the witnesses, and to decide whether to believe some, none or all of what each person said. I thought it must be very hard to be a juror. I mean, I said Bob had sex with me, and he said he didn't. How does the jury decide who's telling the truth and who's telling a lie?

The judge went on to further instruct the jury. He reminded them that Bob was **"presumed innocent."** I shivered when I heard those words. The judge said that the prosecution must prove guilt beyond a "reasonable doubt," but not all doubt.

Then the judge went over the elements of the charges against Bob for the jury to hear, reminding them that Bob was charged with several counts of rape of a child. Then the judge read these things called **statutes.** "Whoever has sexual intercourse or unnatural sexual intercourse . . . abuses a child under the age of sixteen." It all sounded so impersonal, I couldn't believe he was still talking about me. The jury was then told that they had two choices for a verdict: either not guilty, or guilty as charged.

When the judge finished talking to the jury, the court clerk took this wooden box and shook it up. It looked like he was going to draw the winning name for a raffle. I was startled by this familiar, friendly action which seemed so out of place. The clerk chose two names from the box, but instead of winning something, the names identified the alternate jurors. The other twelve jurors left the courtroom and went into the jury room to **deliberate.**

"All rise." The judge swiftly left the courtroom followed by his fluttering black robes. The trial was suddenly over.

I turned to Drew with hope in my eyes and a question in my voice. "It's over?"

"Not yet, Joe," he replied. "It's not over yet."

Section 24

The Verdict

Nina suggested that my parents and I go to the cafeteria in the courthouse for lunch. She didn't want us to go home or leave the courthouse. She wanted us to "stay close" as we waited for the verdict. We went to the cafeteria and ate lunch, although I wasn't very hungry. Then we spent the rest of the afternoon waiting with Drew in the victim/witness waiting room. I swear, I have every single detail of that room memorized!

At exactly 3:39 p.m. Nina appeared in the doorway of the waiting room. The jury had reached a verdict.

And then we were back in the courtroom. I have never in my life been so scared. Drew stayed right beside me the whole time. This was a totally terrible situation. I was feeling panicky because I wasn't sure what I would do if Bob was found "guilty." I wanted him to go to jail. But I worried about that. I couldn't help it. I still loved Bob. But what if he was found "not guilty?" Then everyone would think I was a liar. I had a splitting headache. My teeth were clenched. So were my fists. Drew kept trying to get me to be more relaxed, but there was absolutely no possibility of relaxed!

The jury filed in. The judge appeared. "All rise." I was becoming accustomed to the routine. "This court is now in session." What followed seemed like a dream . . . or a movie. Something unreal, anyway. In fact, if I think about it, I can still play back the entire scene in my mind just as if I were seeing it happen all over again.

The judge spoke. "Women and men of the jury, have you reached a verdict?"

The foreman of the jury stood and replied. "We have."

The clerk asked Bob to stand, and he did. So did his lawyer. And then the verdict. "Guilty as charged." **Guilty as charged** . . . guilty as charged . . . guilty as charged. An echo. I'm sure I heard an echo in the cold, hollow courtroom.

Movement and sound happened slowly and distinctly. I couldn't see Bob's face, but when the guilty verdict was announced, his whole body slumped forward. My face and hands finally relaxed. Bob sat down and held his head in his hands. Was he crying? I was.

The judge spoke. His voice startled me as it filled the hushed courtroom. "The jury is dismissed. The court thanks you for your service. The defendant will be held over for sentencing, which will be in two weeks. This court is adjourned." In that now familiar flurry of swirling black, the judge was gone.

Section 25

After the Trial

In slow motion, I turned to Drew. I looked up at him and whispered, "Is it over?"

"Well, not quite, Joe," he answered. "The trial is over, but the court process is not. In two weeks, at the sentencing hearing, the judge will listen to sentence recommendations from both Nina and Mr. McCarthy. And if you want to say something, there will also be time for you, and your parents, as well, to make a **victim impact statement.** Or, you can write a letter to the judge telling him how you feel about Bob's sentence. In fact, sometimes before the sentencing, people write to the judge on behalf of the defendant, and you need to be prepared for that. Bob may have character witnesses who suggest that he receive **probation** and not be sentenced to jail at all, or that he receive a short sentence."

I just nodded in response, and Drew continued. "I know that you've thought a lot about what kind of sentence you want Bob to receive, Joe. And now is the time for you to decide if you want to make a victim impact statement. You can either say your statement in court the day of the sentencing, or you can write it to the judge. We encourage you and your parents to communicate your feelings to the court in some way, so your voices will be heard. But you don't have to. You don't have to say anything. You don't have to write anything. You don't even have to go to the sentencing hearing. However, I encourage you to let the judge know how important this case is to you."

Drew and I had similar talks before, but hearing it all again put me in a kind of a daze. Maybe I was dazed because I thought it was over. I hoped it was over. I wanted it over. Two more weeks seemed like another eternity, but I knew I'd get through it somehow. I mean, really! Look at what I'd been through already!

During the next days, I spent my time after school alone, going for long walks, mostly. Thinking. I walked and walked, trying very hard to get to the bottom of my feelings about Bob. Talking with Cathy helped, but I knew that getting down to my deep feelings was a solitary activity. And so I walked some more. Finally, after ten days I sat down very late at night and wrote the victim impact statement I wanted to read in the courtroom.

My statement was short. I thought that was best. I honestly didn't know how much I would be able to say.

Section 26

Victim Impact Statement

Since I'm only sixteen years old, I can't know for sure, but I think that being here in this courtroom under these circumstances may be the hardest thing I will ever do in my whole life.

But it's important for me to be here because I want to do everything I can to make sure that Bob can't do to other kids what he did to me. Bob hurt me. He scared me and threatened me. He confused me and used me. He stole things from me that I can never, ever recover. My body was violated and I am so ashamed.

Bob did something wrong, something very wrong. It seems only fair that he should be punished. I don't want him to hurt me or threaten me anymore, or to hurt other kids. I want to feel safe. If Bob is in jail, and can't see me or call me, then maybe I can actually feel safe.

Section 27

Sentencing

The day of the sentencing hearing finally arrived. My parents and Drew and I were sitting in the courtroom at exactly 2:00 p.m., the time the hearing was scheduled. Except for Nina and the court officers, the room was empty. I was nervous and confused. At five minutes past 2:00, more people started coming, but I didn't know who they were. In and out. People kept coming in and going out of the courtroom.

I whispered to Drew a question I had asked him several times before, "What kind of sentence will Bob get?"

"Well," he whispered in reply, "there are guidelines regarding appropriate sentencing for every crime, but the decision in each case is really up to the judge."

At ten minutes past 2:00, more people came in. "Who are these people?" I asked Drew. He told me that other activities were scheduled in court that afternoon. The people were lawyers and victim witness advocates and witnesses and friends and reporters. Some of the people were Bob's friends. I noticed that the lawyers seemed friendly to each other, even if they were on opposite sides. When Mr. McCarthy arrived, Nina shook his hand and spoke to him. I didn't want them to be friendly.

At 2:15, I started going in and out of the courtroom. Getting a drink, going to the bathroom, generally moving around because I was too nervous to sit still. This waiting was so hard. Drew told me that sometimes the waiting is the worst part because it leaves lots of room for apprehension and worry. At that moment, I thought that he was right.

At 2:20, the court officer started talking on his phone and this one lawyer over in the corner was throwing his pen up in the air catching it each time it came down again. Was he nervous, too? Or just passing the time? It seemed to me that nothing at court ever started on time. I wondered if whoever was in charge had any idea how nerve-racking all this waiting was. My heart was pounding so hard, that I worried I might be having a heart attack. But I wasn't.

Finally, people slowly began taking their places. They sat down one by one and became quiet. Bob was brought in, and he sat on the other side of the courtroom. He didn't look at me.

"All rise." The judge appeared. "Be seated. This court is now in session." A solemn quiet. The clerk announced the other cases, stated who was present and who the lawyers were. Now things seemed to happen very quickly, and soon the courtroom was nearly empty.

The clerk announced our case and acknowledged Nina and Mr. Mc-Carthy as the lawyers. Bob went forward and sat next to Mr. McCarthy.

Then Nina stood. I stopped breathing. Nina spoke directly to the judge. Her voice was clear and loud. It echoed in the solemn space. "Thank you, Your Honor. On behalf of the commonwealth, the district attorney's office recommends a state prison sentence. The planned and manipulated sexual abuse of children is the most disgusting and heinous crime. Bob is a pro at this type of abuse. And as it has been proved in this court of law, he is a sophisticated, deliberate and aggressive abuser of children. He has made Joe's life into a living nightmare. Joe was a helpless, defenseless, appreciative child, and he suffered the ultimate betrayal of a trusted, adult friend and caretaker. Nothing we do here today can totally heal Joe's wounds. However, what we can do is hold Bob responsible for his crimes. We cannot even guess at the number of children Bob has victimized, but we do know he has been actively abusing boys in the neighborhoods of our county for years. Bob was found guilty of the sexual abuse of this victim by a jury of his peers. Although we cannot take away Joe's suffering, we can send a message to all child molesters, through this molester, that our society will not tolerate the mistreatment of our children. Therefore, the commonwealth recommends a state prison sentence, to be followed by a **suspended sentence** from and after the committed sentence, during which time sex offender counseling will be mandatory."

When Nina was finished there was a hush over the courtroom. It was my turn to speak. I walked up to the witness stand and sat down. I unfolded my paper and looked at Nina and then at the judge. I looked at my parents. I looked at Drew. Then I looked at Bob. Whew, that was hard. I thought he might look at me, but instead he stared at some papers on the table in front of him. I read my statement, grateful that it was short, because I almost started to cry. This whole situation was a terrible nightmare. I still couldn't believe it was all happening.

I finished my statement, folded up my paper and went back to my place next to Drew. Then my dad took the stand. He had prepared an impact statement to read to the court. Dad's statement was a lot longer than mine. He told the court about my fear, about how I wondered how old I would be when Bob got out of jail. How I wondered if I would be able to protect myself from him. How I wondered if I'd always be afraid. Dad talked about how ashamed I was because of being sexual with Bob. Then my dad got choked up as he asked the court to "respect the bravery of my son." As Dad continued, his voice was kind of shaky. "Joe is just a kid, a kid acting and speaking in the face of fear for his own safety, and in the fear of public shame, to protect other kids. He has come forward at great cost to himself, a cost that I don't think we as adults can imagine. How dare this man harm this boy, my son!"

I thought Dad was going to cry. I couldn't help myself. I did cry.

Dad continued. "How dare he! I have watched and supported my son as he dealt with the legal system, knowing how hard it was for him, knowing the pain it was causing him, knowing that it was the only rational way to deal with this. And the legal system has worked. Bob has been convicted. And now I ask the court to ensure that what my son has tired to do, does, in fact, come to pass. Protect other kids from Bob by removing him from access to kids for as long as possible."

When Dad stopped talking no one moved for a minute or so. It seemed that no one was even breathing. Then Dad looked at the judge and said, "Thank you. Thank you for this opportunity to speak." Dad had tears in his eyes.

Dad returned to his seat next to me, and the sentencing hearing continued. Mr. McCarthy spoke on Bob's behalf. "He is not a one-dimensional person. We cannot deny him his humanity. He has been a responsible citizen. The judge has received a number of letters from friends and relatives who have known him for more than twenty years. He has a friendly, generous spirit . . . " Mr. McCarthy went on and on saying what a great guy Bob was. It was hard for me to believe that Nina and Mr. McCarthy were talking about the same person.

And then the judge talked, for what seemed like a really long time before he got to the sentencing. Finally, he asked Bob to stand. Then the clerk announced the sentence. "You have been found guilty . . .

you are sentenced to a prison term in the state prison . . . to be followed by a suspended sentence . . . will include mandatory counseling . . . sentence to begin immediately." The court officers came up to Bob and led him away through a mysterious door in the back of the courtroom. Drew said that door led to the jail.

As I watched Bob walk away time stopped for me. Shocked, stunned. I don't know. A shiver went through my whole body. People were talking to me, but I couldn't hear them. I was stunned, I guess. Drew steered my parents and me out of the courtroom and into the victim/witness waiting room. I sat down, relieved, exhausted, grateful that Bob couldn't hurt me or those little guys I saw getting into his van. He couldn't hurt any kids anymore.

Well, the trial was finally over. Now the part about putting my life back together was about to begin.

Section 28

Toward Recovery

It hasn't even been two years since I first told Mr. Stone about the sexual abuse, but it seems like it all happened centuries ago. The investigation and trial sort of happened in addition to my regular life, and now that the trial is over, I want to pick up my life where I left off.

In some ways I feel lucky. Not lucky that Bob abused me. He asked me to do things I was not ready to do, and then I had to deal with the court process, which I really was not equipped to deal with. Bob was a fright in my life. He was destructive. But I do feel lucky because there are people who care about kids. And I'm grateful that those people helped me. In fact, they still help me. I see Cathy every week, and probably will keep seeing her for awhile. She has helped me to understand the experience of sexual abuse and to work on my feelings about it. Sorting out my feelings can be very, very hard work, and will "take some time" Cathy said. I mostly hate doing this "work," but then the upset and the work seem worth it when I finally come to understand more about my experience and to accept it.

I feel sad and angry every time I think about Bob. He was a great friend. We had such good times. But still, what he did—I don't think I can ever forgive him for that. I don't think I want to forgive him. You know, he never ever said he was sorry. I sure hope Bob learns something while he is in jail. I hope he understands how much he hurt me and all the other kids he abused over the years. I hope he understands that what he did was wrong and that he can never sexually abuse a child, ever again.

Given what I've been through in my life so far, things are going as well as can be expected. I'm doing okay in school, I guess. My grades aren't bad, and in the spring I'm planning to try out for the track team. Mr. Stone is the coach. I've even dated a little, very little, but enough to realize that I have a lot to learn about relationships and sex.

"But doesn't everyone!" Cathy said.

Sometimes it's tempting to think about burying my past and my pain with drugs and alcohol, like some kids at school do, but I resist. I know that keeping things buried won't help me much in the long run. Sometimes I have the worst nightmares that just won't end. Sometimes I'm tired, real tired. Sometimes I'm sick. I still have a lot of headaches. Sometimes life isn't exactly fun for me. But now, at least, I know I'm in control of my own body and my own life. It was so important to come forward and stop Bob. My dad told me that by coming forward like I did took as much courage as he has ever seen in his life. And my dad has been with a lot of courageous people, like when he was in Vietnam. My parents' support meant so much to me. They didn't blame me for what happened. They were proud of me for coming forward and stopping Bob.

In a way, I'm sorry I can't end this story by telling you that I "lived happily ever after." But I'm only sixteen years old, so this isn't anywhere near the end. Anyway, that happily ever after stuff is for kids and fairy tales. This is real life, my life. And in a way, it's the beginning of the best part of my life. Oh, I'll never forget what Bob did, and I'll never forget the pain. But I'm going to keep working at understanding myself and what happened, because I firmly believe that with work and persistence, life will be better. I have lots of hope for the future thanks to Mr. Stone and Patrick O'Neill and Drew and Nina and Cathy and my parents . . . well, you know, thanks to everyone who helped me and everyone who cared.

Guiding Questions

Section 1. I'm Joe

1. Do you remember how old you were when the abuse you experienced started?
2. When and how did you realize that what was happening to you was abuse?
3. What feelings and reactions did you experience while the abuse was happening?
4. Joe had confusing feelings about Bob, his abuser. Did/do you have confusing feelings about your abuser? What are some of your feelings?

Section 2. The First Time I Told

1. How did you decide to tell someone about the abuse?
2. Whom did you first tell? What was helpful about his or her reaction?
3. After he told Mr. Stone about the abuse, Joe felt a mixture of feelings: shame, guilt, confusion, sadness. These are *some* of the feelings teens experience after disclosing about abuse. What feelings did you experience after you told?
4. Did the person you told notify anyone else? If so, how did/do you feel about other people knowing?
5. How did you feel about yourself after disclosing the abuse?

Section 3. I'm Sorry

1. Sometimes parents are supportive and helpful to an abused teen, as Joe's parents were. Sometimes their initial reactions, such as Joe's dad's anger, can be scary. Sometimes parents and other family members are too upset about the abuse and worried about what will happen to be supportive of the teen. What was it like for you when your parents first learned about the abuse?

2. Did you know that your state had a Mandated Reporter Law regarding child abuse? How did/do you feel about your abuse being reported to the social service and legal authorities?

Section 4. Making a Report

1. Joe's guidance counselor gave him a telephone number for a twenty-four-hour crisis line. How do you think that calling the crisis line would have helped Joe? How do you think it would help you to call a crisis line?
2. Joe worried that if the kids at school found out about the abuse and that he told about Bob, they would think he was "weird" or "a snitch" or "damaged." Did/do you have similar worries? Are you worried about additional things kids might think about you if they knew?
3. After his disclosure and the abuse was reported, Joe's feelings became very intense. He tried to manage his feelings by retreating to his room, listening to music, watching TV, playing basketball, and not talking about the situation. What do you do to help manage intense feelings?
4. Crying was difficult and embarrassing for Joe. How do you feel about boys crying?

Section 5. The Investigation Begins

1. Why do you think that the person who abused you did it?
2. How did/do you feel about telling more people about the abuse?
3. How did/do you think that your friends and relatives and teachers and other people you know will feel about you after they find out about the abuse?
4. Joe didn't want to have to tell more people about the abuse, but he knew it was important to tell in order to stop Bob from abusing more boys. How do you feel about taking steps to stop your abuser from abusing other kids?

Section 6. The Interview

1. What were some of the feelings you experienced before, during, and after your interview?
2. How did/do you feel about saying exactly what happened to you?

3. Joe felt ashamed saying words such as penis and anus. What words are hard for you to say?
4. Joe felt proud of himself for being strong enough to do something to stop Bob even though he was scared to do it. How do you feel about yourself when you do something that is very hard for you to do?

Section 7. After the Interview

1. The investigation and prosecution processes were confusing to Joe because they were all new and different. If the processes seem confusing to you or your family, what can you do to help yourself better understand what is happening?
2. What do you want to happen to your abuser if he or she is found guilty?
3. How will you feel if your abuser is found not guilty?
4. How do you feel about not knowing what the outcome of the case will be?
5. How do you feel about the possibility of your abuser being arrested?
6. What opinions do you and members of your family have about counseling?

Section 8. Counseling

1. How did you feel (physically and emotionally) before you told people about the abuse? How did you feel after you told?
2. Do you think you would call a therapist or a crisis line if you wanted or needed to talk with someone? Why? Why not?
3. Joe made a list of items to talk about with his therapist, Cathy. How do you feel about the items on Joe's list? How is your list the same and different? Write a list of items you want to talk about or know more about.

Section 9. Prosecution Begins

1. Sometimes it is not a good idea for a victim of child sexual abuse to go forward with prosecution. How will you know if it is a good idea for you to go forward?
2. What do you think about the concept that someone accused of a crime is considered innocent until proven guilty?

3. What are some of the words or practices in the criminal justice system that you find confusing?

Section 10. Pretrial Testimony

1. How has the fact of your abuse affected other members of your family?
2. How was the interview handled in your case? How did/do you feel about this process?
3. What was/is the hardest thing for you to talk about regarding the abuse?
4. What helps you trust that you can count on people to be there for you?

Section 11. Counseling Support

1. How were/are you feeling about your abuser after your disclosure and during the investigation process?
2. Who can you talk with about any feelings you have that are difficult for you or that you do not understand?
3. How do you feel about having the power to stop the prosecution at any time?

Section 12. Waiting

1. What information do you need to help you better understand why the court process takes so long?
2. Waiting is difficult for most people. How do you cope with waiting?

Section 13. At School

1. What kind of support do you need at school? How can you ask for what you need?
2. How did people in your life (friends, family, teachers) react when they learned that you had been sexually abused? Which reactions were helpful? Which ones hurt you? Why?
3. How do you know whom to trust?

Section 14. The Indictment

1. How do you feel about the possibility that your abuser's name will appear in the newspaper and on television?
2. What do the laws in your state say about keeping the victim's name private? (*Note:* You can check with your state legislator's office for this information, or ask your victim witness advocate.)

Section 15. The Arraignment

1. How do you feel about the amount of time your case is taking?
2. Do you understand the reasons for any delays? What are they?
3. What kind of support do you need to help you through this long process?
4. Are there any words in this chapter that you don't understand? (*Note:* The vocabulary used in court and about the court process is unique. Consult the glossary and ask questions any time you do not understand a word.)

Section 16. Waiting Again

1. How do you feel about the possibility of your abuser contacting you or trying to see you?
2. If you feel afraid of your abuser, what steps have been taken to keep you safe?
3. If you think it's a good idea to put your troubles aside sometimes, how do you do that?

Section 17. The Empty Courtroom

1. What do you think it means to prove the defendant's guilt beyond a reasonable doubt?
2. How will you feel if your abuser is acquitted (found not guilty) by the jury? How will you feel if your abuser is convicted (found guilty)?
3. Do you think it is a good idea to visit the empty courtroom before the trial? Would you like to do this? Why? Why not?

Section 18. Pretrial Details

1. Sometimes judges will make minor accommodations for young victims and witnesses. Sometimes they will not make accommodations. But, it is important to ask for whatever you need to help make the process less stressful for you. What kind of accommodations do you think will be helpful to you in court? Why? Have you discussed accommodations with your victim witness advocate? Have you asked what accommodations in the courtroom have been allowed and helpful to other kids?
2. When Joe got upset about the court process, he wondered, "Whose side are they on?" Sometimes abuse victims feel revictimized by the court process. How do you feel about how your case is being handled?

Section 19. Delays and Preparations

1. How do you feel when you are informed about delays in the trial date?
2. There will be months of waiting before the trial begins. What can you do while you are waiting for the trial to start to help yourself feel prepared?

Section 20. The Trial Begins

1. How did/do you feel about the trial finally starting?
2. The experience of being in court will be different for each victim and witness. What was/is the trial like for you? What part of the experience surprised you the most? What part did/do you dislike the most?

Section 21. In Court

1. The courtroom is a tense place, and the beginning of a trial sparks intense emotions. What feelings do/did you have as you anticipate(d) the trial?
2. Were there parts of the trial that you did not understand or that you found particularly upsetting? (For example, the number of jurors, or the sequestering of witnesses, or the court being open to the public.) Who can you ask to help you better understand

the process and/or to support you through upsetting experiences?

3. Testifying before open court is stressful for everyone—even adults. How can you be prepared for this stress, and how can you take good care of yourself after testifying?

4. Did any unusual circumstances or events take place during your trial? How did you cope with these?

Section 22. Cross-Examination

1. The purpose of cross-examination is to cast doubt on the witness's testimony. This can be confusing and upsetting. What do you think will be the hardest part about being cross-examined? What can you do to be prepared?

2. How will you feel if the defense attorney says that you imagined the abuse or lied about the abuse? What kind of support do you need to deal with this possibility? Would it be better for you to not hear the closing arguments? Why?

Section 23. Instructions to the Jury

1. How do you determine if someone is telling the truth or lying?

2. How do you think members of a jury go about determining who is telling the truth and who is lying?

Section 24. The Verdict

1. Even after going through the investigation and the trial, Joe was not sure about what he wanted the verdict to be. How do you feel about the verdict your abuser received?

2. Are you surprised at all by your feelings? Why? Why not?

Section 25. After the Trial

1. How do you feel about being able to tell the judge what sentence you think your abuser should receive?

2. How do you think you can best figure out what you want to happen to your abuser?

Section 26. Victim Impact Statement

1. How do you feel about the abuse that happened to you? How do you feel about your abuser?
2. What have been the effects of the abuse on your life so far?
3. What do you want your abuser's sentence to be?
4. How will writing (or not writing) a victim impact statement be helpful to you?

Section 27. Sentencing

1. What was the day of the sentencing like for you?
2. How do you think you will feel when you hear the prosecutor say negative things about your abuser and the defense attorney say positive things about your abuser?
3. How do you feel about helping to make sure that your abuser is held responsible for his or her abusive behavior?
4. How do you feel about helping to protect other kids?

Section 28. Toward Recovery

1. How do you feel about forgiving your abuser?
2. What do you want people to know about the experience you have been through? About the abuse? About the trial?
3. What do you want people to know about how these experiences have changed you—for better? for worse?
4. Who are the people you want to thank for helping you through this process? What do you want to say to them?

SUPPORT PEOPLE I CAN DEPEND ON

	Name	Telephone #
Therapist/Counselor		
24-Hour Crisis Line		
Victim Witness Advocate		
Child Interview Specialist		
Assistant District Attorney		
Police Officer		
Doctor		
Friend		
Friend		

HOW IT HAPPENED FOR ME: A DIAGRAM

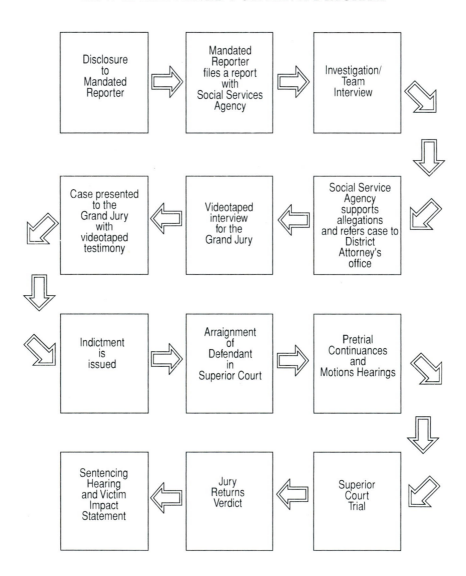

Glossary

acquitted: The charges against the defendant have been dismissed. Most often, if a defendant is acquitted, it is as a result of the jury finding the defendant "not guilty."

ADA: Assistant District Attorney.

allegation: A stated or written accusation by a victim of what happened.

arraignment: The beginning step of the trial proceedings. The defendant comes to court and is formally read the charges.

assistant district attorney (ADA): Lawyer or prosecutor who works for the state (or commonwealth) and represents the state (or commonwealth) on behalf of a crime victim. (*Note:* Check in the following list to see what the prosecuting attorney is called in your state.) *Alabama*, District Attorney; *Alaska*, District Attorney; *Arizona*, County Attorney; *Arkansas*, Prosecuting Attorney; *California*, District Attorney; *Colorado*, District Attorney; *Connecticut*, State's Attorney; *Delaware*, Attorney General; *District of Columbia (Washington, D.C.)*, U.S. Attorney; *Florida*, State Attorney; *Georgia*, District Attorney; *Hawaii*, Prosecuting Attorney; *Idaho*, Prosecuting Attorney; *Illinois*, State's Attorney; *Indiana*, Prosecuting Attorney; *Iowa*, County Attorney; *Kansas*, District Attorney or County Attorney; *Kentucky*, Commonwealth's Attorney or County Attorney; *Louisiana*, District Attorney; *Maine*, District Attorney; *Maryland*, State's Attorney; *Massachusetts*, District Attorney; *Michigan*, Prosecuting Attorney; *Minnesota*, County Attorney; *Mississippi*, District Attorney or County Attorney; *Missouri*, Prosecuting Attorney; *Montana*, County Attorney; *Nebraska*, County Attorney; *Nevada*, District Attorney; *New Hampshire*, County Attorney; *New Jersey*, County Prosecutor; *New Mexico*, District Attorney; *New York*, District Attorney; *North Carolina*, District Attorney; *North Dakota*, State's Attorney; *Ohio*, Prosecuting Attorney; *Oklahoma*, District Attorney; *Oregon*,

District Attorney; *Pennsylvania,* District Attorney; *Rhode Island,* Attorney General; *South Carolina,* Circuit Solicitor; *South Dakota,* State's Attorney; *Tennessee,* District Attorney General; *Texas,* Criminal District Attorney or County/District Attorney or District Attorney or County Attorney; *Utah,* County Attorney; *Vermont,* State's Attorney; *Virginia,* Commonwealth's Attorney; *Washington,* County Prosecuting Attorney; *West Virginia,* County Prosecuting Attorney; *Wisconsin,* County District Attorney; *Wyoming,* District Attorney or County Attorney or Prosecuting Attorney. (*National Directory of Prosecuting Attorneys,* 2001. Arlington, VA: National District Attorney's Association, pp. 89-97).

bail: The amount of money posted as a guarantee that the defendant will appear in court on all of the specified court dates.

bail hearing: Hearing in court before a judge to decide whether bail should be posted or whether a defendant can be released on his or her own personal recognizance.

burden of proof: By law, the prosecution is completely responsible for proving a defendant guilty in court "beyond a reasonable doubt." The defendant does not have to prove that he or she is innocent, does not have to testify, and does not even have to have any witnesses testify.

character witness: A person (such as a relative, friend, or employer) who knows the defendant well enough to testify about his or her character; that is about what a good person he or she is and what positive traits he or she has (such as honesty, loyalty, compassion, etc.).

child interview specialist: A person trained to ask children and teenagers questions about what happened in a skillful and sensitive way.

closing arguments: The arguments presented by the prosecutor and the defense attorney at the end of the trial. Each lawyer attempts to convince the jury how to decide based on the evidence presented.

complaining witness: The victim.

continuance: A decision by the court to review the case at a later date.

convicted: The defendant has been found guilty as charged by a jury or a judge.

counselor: A helping professional who listens to you and provides support and information about your feelings.

court officers: Officers of the court who make sure the court operates in an orderly way. Like police officers, the court officers wear uniforms and make sure that all the people in court remain safe.

court reporter: The person who makes a record of everything said in the courtroom. The record can be made by speaking into a machine or by typing into a machine, or both.

credibility: The issue of whether or not an individual's statements are believable.

criminal justice system: A system of government consisting of different types of professionals (judges, district attorneys, police officers, parole and probation officers, victim witness advocates, child interview specialists) which is designed to protect the public, and to work with both victims and perpetrators of crimes.

crisis line: A twenty-four-hour emergency telephone service providing support, counseling and information.

cross-examine: An opportunity for the opposing lawyer to ask a witness questions about evidence which has already been presented to the court.

defendant: The person charged with committing a crime.

defense attorney: A lawyer who represents the defendant.

deliberate: When the jury goes into a private room after a trial is over and discusses all of the evidence from the trial, and decides the verdict. A superior court jury needs to be unanimous in their decision, which means that all twelve jurors must agree on the same verdict.

disclosure: A statement made by a person relating the details of an incident or incidents of abuse.

disposition: The final outcome of a court case. This word often refers to the sentence a defendant receives.

DSS (Department of Social Services): Agency mandated by the Commonwealth of Massachusetts to receive and respond to reports of child abuse and neglect, to provide protection to children, and to provide services to children and their families. (*Note:* Check in the following list to see what the child protective agency is called in your state.) *Alabama,* Office of Protective Services; Adult, Child and Family Services Division; Department of Human Resources; *Alaska,* Division of Family and Youth Services; Department of Health and Social Services; *Arizona,* Administration for Children, Youth, and Families; Department of Economic Security; *Arkansas,* Division of Children and Family Services; Department of Human Services; *California,* Department of Social Services; *Colorado,* Department of Human Services; *Connecticut,* Division of Children and Protective Services; Department of Children and Families; *Delaware,* Division of Family Services; Department of Services to Children, Youth, and Their Families; *District of Columbia,* Child and Family Services; Department of Human Services; *Florida,* Department of Children and Family; *Georgia,* Division of Children and Family Services; Department of Human Resources; *Guam,* Child Protective Services, Child Welfare Services; Department of Public Health and Social Services; *Hawaii,* Family and Adult Services; Department of Human Services; *Idaho,* Division of Family and Community Services; Department of Health and Welfare; *Illinois,* Department of Children and Family Services; *Indiana,* Family and Social Services Administration; *Iowa,* Adult, Children and Family Services; Department of Human Services; *Kansas,* Children and Family Services; Department of Social and Rehabilitative Services; *Kentucky,* Department for Protection and Family Support; Cabinet for Families and Children; *Louisiana,* Department of Social Services; *Maine,* Child Protective Services; Department of Human Services; *Maryland,* Child Protective Services; Department of Human Resources; *Massachusetts,* Department of Social Services; *Michigan,* Child Protective Services Division; Department of Social Services; *Minnesota,* Department of Human Services; *Mississippi,* Child Protective Services Unit; Division of Family and Children's Services; Department of Human Services; *Missouri,* Division of Family Services; Department of Social Services; *Montana,* Child and Family Services Division; Department of Public Health and Human Services; *Nebraska,* Department of Health and Human Services; *Nevada,* Division of Child and Family Services; Department of Human Resources; *New Hampshire,* Division for Children, Youth, and Families; Department of Health and Human Services; *New Jersey,* Division of Youth and Family Services; *New*

Mexico, Children, Youth and Families Department; *New York,* Division of Family and Children Services; Department of Social Services; *North Carolina,* Child Protective Services; Division of Social Services, Department of Human Resources; *North Dakota,* Child Protection Services; Department of Human Services; *Ohio,* Office of Child Care and Family Services; Department of Human Services; *Oklahoma,* Division of Children, Youth, and Family; Department of Human Services; *Oregon,* Child Protective Services; State Office for Services to Children and Families, Department of Human Resources; *Pennsylvania,* Office of Children, Youth, and Families; Department of Public Welfare; *Puerto Rico,* Families with Children Program; Department of Social Services; *Rhode Island,* Division of Child Protective Services; Department of Children, Youth, and Families; *South Carolina,* Child Protective Services; Department of Social Services; *South Dakota,* Child Protection Services; Department of Social Services; *Tennessee,* Child Protective Services; Department of Children's Services, Department of Human Services; *Texas,* Department of Protective and Regulatory Services; Department of Human Services; *Utah,* Division of Family Services; Department of Human Services; *Vermont,* Department of Social and Rehabilitative Services; *Virgin Islands,* Division of Children, Youth, and Families; Department of Human Services; *Virginia,* Child Protective Services; Department of Social Services; *Washington,* Child Protective Services; Children's Administration; Department of Social and Health Services; *West Virginia,* Office of Social Services; Department of Health and Human Resources; *Wisconsin,* Child Protective Services; Division of Children and Family Services; Department of Health and Social Services; *Wyoming,* Department of Family Services (U.S. Department of Health and Human Services, 1992; U.S. Department of Health and Human Services, 1998).

empaneling: To select a jury.

Fifth Amendment: The United States Constitution provides rights to people accused of crimes. One of those rights, which is contained in the Fifth Amendment, states that persons accused of crimes do not have to say anything that could be used against them in court.

grand jury: A group of up to twenty-three people who hear evidence and decide whether or not there is reasonable cause to believe a crime happened. Twelve members of the grand jury (a majority) must agree that there is reasonable cause.

guilty: A determination which indicates that the state prosecutor has successfully presented the facts in a way that met the burden of proof beyond a reasonable doubt.

guilty as charged: The decision of the jury that the defendant is guilty of the particular charge specified by the indictment.

indictment: The name used for the formal criminal charge against the defendant.

interview: A meeting with a child interview specialist to talk about what happened.

investigation: The process during which professionals from different disciplines (therapists, child interview specialists, social workers, lawyers, police officers) gather the facts about what happened.

judge: The person who is authorized to hear cases in court and make sure the court is run in an orderly manner.

judge's clerk: The judge's assistant. The clerk sits at a desk in front of the judge and helps the judge run the court by swearing people in as witnesses, keeping track of case documents, and reading verdicts.

jury: A group of up to sixteen people who listen to the facts of the case. Twelve selected jurors will then decide if the defendant is guilty of the charges beyond a reasonable doubt.

mandated reporter: A number of professionals including doctors, therapists, teachers, police officers, foster parents, guidance counselors, or any other person who cares for or works with children in any public or private facility.

mandated reporting law: Requires certain professionals (known as mandated reporters) to file a report when, in his or her professional capacity, he or she has reasonable cause to suspect that a child under the age of eighteen (age varies by state) has been or is being physically or sexually abused or neglected. (*Note:* Investigate the mandated reporting law in your state to see who the mandated reporters are and other points of interest in the law. Every state has a mandated reporting law regarding child abuse.)

motions hearings: *See* PRETRIAL CONFERENCES.

not guilty: A determination which indicates that the state prosecutor has not met the burden of proof beyond a reasonable doubt. This determination does not mean the defendant is innocent.

opening statement: The opportunity for both the prosecutor and the defense attorney to present an outline of what they will accomplish during the trial.

plead: To state on the record whether one is guilty or not guilty of the charges.

presumed innocent: Even after a person has been arrested or charged with a crime, the law says that the accused person must be considered innocent until the prosecution proves him or her guilty.

pretrial conferences: Meetings in court to decide what will happen next on the case. The judge, prosecuting attorney, defendant, and defense attorney take part in the conferences. Victims and witnesses do not have to be present in court. There may be several pretrial conference dates scheduled in court before a trial date is finally scheduled.

pretrial motions: Court appearances by both the prosecuting attorney and the defense attorney before the trial begins in order to discuss the preparation of the case with the judge.

probable cause hearing: In states where the grand jury system is not used, this hearing takes place before a judge for the purpose of determining if the prosecuting attorney has enough evidence of the defendant's guilt to move forward to a jury trial.

probation: A kind of sentence in which the defendant is required to follow rules outlined and monitored by a probation officer. For example: having to go to counseling, meeting with a probation officer regularly, staying away from children. Sometimes a defendant is given probation instead of a prison sentence and sometimes probation is given in addition to a prison sentence. If a defendant does not follow the rules of probation, a judge can then order the defendant to go to jail.

prosecution: A process by which the state (commonwealth) brings criminal charges against someone, and then brings a case to trial.

reasonable doubt: Any doubt that a reasonable, responsible person would have a hard time dismissing.

recess: A break in the trial proceedings.

restraining order: An order issued by a judge specifying that one individual be prevented from abusing another individual, and be kept away from and/or removed from the premises of the person who applied for the restraining order.

sequestered: To be separated, so as not to be influenced by the testimony of one another. A jury can also be sequestered so as not to be influenced by the media.

social worker: A professional trained to provide a range of services to families including support and counseling.

statutes: Laws that are created by the state or federal government.

subpoena: A court order sent to a witness, requiring the witness to be present in court. A subpoena can be sent by mail or delivered by hand by a constable, sheriff, or agent of the court.

summons: A written notification issued by the court that orders the defendant to appear in court on a certain day to be arraigned. A summons can be sent by mail or delivered by hand.

superior court: The level of the court system that handles more serious crimes known as felonies. (*Note:* Some child abuse cases are tried in the district court system. This could be because the crime is considered a misdemeanor [which is a less serious crime—like indecent exposure] instead of a felony. District court procedures will differ from those in superior court. If your case is going through the district court system, be sure to ask your victim witness advocate to explain the different procedures.)

supported the allegations: To support an allegation of abuse means that the state social service agency has reasonable cause to believe that an incident of abuse or neglect of a child or teenager did occur.

suspended sentence: A prison sentence that a defendant is not required to serve right away. Instead the defendant is placed on probation with certain rules that must be followed. Usually these rules include sex-offender treatment and no contact with the victim. If the defendant does not follow the rules of probation, he or she could be made to serve the suspended sentence in prison.

team interview: A team of professionals consisting of a social worker, assistant district attorney, victim witness advocate, child interview specialist, police officer, and a therapist who come together to cooperatively conduct an investigation, including observing an interview and discussing what should happen next in the case.

testify: To answer questions in court under the oath to tell the truth.

testimony: A statement made by a witness under oath in response to questions asked by a lawyer.

therapist: A person trained to assist others in dealing with problems or concerns.

verdict: The decision of the jury. In a superior court criminal trial the decision must be unanimous.

victim: The person who is wronged by the crime.

victim impact statement: At the time of sentencing victims and their families can make a written or a verbal statement to the judge about how they feel about what happened, what the effects of the crime are, and what they think the sentence should be. In deciding what sentence a defendant will receive, the judge considers what the prosecuting attorney, the defense attorney, and the victims recommend.

victim witness advocate: A support person who guides victims and witnesses through the court system.

warrant: A document authorizing the arrest of the defendant.

witness: A person who testifies (tells), under oath, what he or she saw or heard happen.

witness stand: The place in court where the witness sits or stands to testify. At this place, usually next to the judge, the witness will be sworn in and will answer questions.

THE HAWORTH MALTREATMENT AND TRAUMA PRESS®
Robert A. Geffner, PhD
Senior Editor

THE INSIDERS: A MAN'S RECOVERY FROM TRAUMATIC CHILDHOOD ABUSE by Robert Blackburn Knight. (2002). "An important book. . . . Fills a gap in the literature about healing from childhood sexual abuse by allowing us to hear, in undiluted terms, about one man's history and journey of recovery." *Amy Pine, MA, LMFT, psychotherapist and co-founder, Survivors Healing Center, Santa Cruz, California*

WE ARE NOT ALONE: A GUIDEBOOK FOR HELPING PROFESSIONALS AND PARENTS SUPPORTING ADOLESCENT VICTIMS OF SEXUAL ABUSE by Jade Christine Angelica. (2002). "Encourages victims and their families to participate in the system in an effort to heal from their victimization, seek justice, and hold offenders accountable for their crimes. An exceedingly vital training tool." *Janet Fine, MS, Director, Victim Witness Assistance Program and Children's Advocacy Center, Suffolk County District Attorney's Office, Boston*

WE ARE NOT ALONE: A TEENAGE GIRL'S PERSONAL ACCOUNT OF INCEST FROM DISCLOSURE THROUGH PROSECUTION AND TREATMENT by Jade Christine Angelica. (2002). "A valuable resource for teens who have been sexually abused and their parents. With compassion and eloquent prose, Angelica walks people through the criminal justice system—from disclosure to final outcome." *Kathleen Kendall-Tackett, PhD, Research Associate, Family Research Laboratory, University of New Hampshire, Durham*

WE ARE NOT ALONE: A TEENAGE BOY'S PERSONAL ACCOUNT OF CHILD SEXUAL ABUSE FROM DISCLOSURE THROUGH PROSECUTION AND TREATMENT by Jade Christine Angelica. (2002). "Inspires us to work harder to meet kids' needs, answer their questions, calm their fears, and protect them from their abusers and the system, which is often not designed to respond to them in a language they understand." *Kevin L. Ryle, JD, Assistant District Attorney, Middlesex, Massachusetts*

GROWING FREE: A MANUAL FOR SURVIVORS OF DOMESTIC VIOLENCE by Wendy Susan Deaton and Michael Hertica. (2001). "This is a necessary book for anyone who is scared and starting to think about what it would take to 'grow free.' . . . Very helpful for friends and relatives of a person in a domestic violence situation. I recommend it highly." *Colleen Friend, LCSW, Field Work Consultant, UCLA Department of Social Welfare, School of Public Policy & Social Research*

A THERAPIST'S GUIDE TO **GROWING FREE: A MANUAL FOR SURVIVOR'S OF DOMESTIC VIOLENCE** by Wendy Susan Deaton and Michael Hertica. (2001). "An excellent synopsis of the theories and research behind the manual." *Beatrice Crofts Yorker, RN, JD, Professor of Nursing, Georgia State University, Decatur*

PATTERNS OF CHILD ABUSE: HOW DYSFUNCTIONAL TRANSACTIONS ARE REPLICATED IN INDIVIDUALS, FAMILIES, AND THE CHILD WELFARE SYSTEM by Michael Karson. (2001). "No one interested in what may well be the major public health epidemic of our time in terms of its long-term consequences for our society can afford to pass up the opportunity to read this enlightening work." *Howard Wolowitz, PhD, Professor Emeritus, Psychology Department, University of Michigan, Ann Arbor*

IDENTIFYING CHILD MOLESTERS: PREVENTING CHILD SEXUAL ABUSE BY RECOGNIZING THE PATTERNS OF THE OFFENDERS by Carla van Dam. (2000). "The definitive work on the subject. . . . Provides parents and others with the tools to recognize when and how to intervene." *Roger W. Wolfe, MA, Co-Director, N. W. Treatment Associates, Seattle, Washington*

POLITICAL VIOLENCE AND THE PALESTINIAN FAMILY: IMPLICATIONS FOR MENTAL HEALTH AND WELL-BEING by Vivian Khamis. (2000). "A valuable book . . . a pioneering work that fills a glaring gap in the study of Palestinian society." *Elia Zureik, Professor of Sociology, Queens University, Kingston, Ontario, Canada*

STOPPING THE VIOLENCE: A GROUP MODEL TO CHANGE MEN'S ABUSIVE ATTITUDES AND BEHAVIORS by David J. Decker. (1999). "A concise and thorough manual to assist clinicians in learning the causes and dynamics of domestic violence." *Joanne Kittel, MSW, LICSW, Yachats, Oregon*

STOPPING THE VIOLENCE: A GROUP MODEL TO CHANGE MEN'S ABUSIVE ATTITUDES AND BEHAVIORS, THE CLIENT WORKBOOK by David J. Decker. (1999).

BREAKING THE SILENCE: GROUP THERAPY FOR CHILDHOOD SEXUAL ABUSE, A PRACTITIONER'S MANUAL by Judith A. Margolin. (1999). "This book is an extremely valuable and well-written resource for all therapists working with adult survivors of child sexual abuse." *Esther Deblinger, PhD, Associate Professor of Clinical Psychiatry, University of Medicine and Dentistry of New Jersey School of Osteopathic Medicine*

"I NEVER TOLD ANYONE THIS BEFORE": MANAGING THE INITIAL DISCLOSURE OF SEXUAL ABUSE RE-COLLECTIONS by Janice A. Gasker. (1999). "Discusses the elements needed to create a safe, therapeutic environment and offers the practitioner a number of useful strategies for responding appropriately to client disclosure." *Roberta G. Sands, PhD, Associate Professor, University of Pennsylvania School of Social Work*

FROM SURVIVING TO THRIVING: A THERAPIST'S GUIDE TO STAGE II RECOVERY FOR SURVIVORS OF CHILDHOOD ABUSE by Mary Bratton. (1999). "A must read for all, including survivors. Bratton takes a lifelong debilitating disorder and unravels its intricacies in concise, succinct, and understandable language." *Phillip A. Whitner, PhD, Sr. Staff Counselor, University Counseling Center, The University of Toledo, Ohio*

SIBLING ABUSE TRAUMA: ASSESSMENT AND INTERVENTION STRAT-EGIES FOR CHILDREN, FAMILIES, AND ADULTS by John V. Caffaro and Allison Conn-Caffaro. (1998). "One area that has almost consistently been ignored in the research and writing on child maltreatment is the area of sibling abuse. This book is a welcome and required addition to the developing literature on abuse." *Judith L. Alpert, PhD, Professor of Applied Psychology, New York University*

BEARING WITNESS: VIOLENCE AND COLLECTIVE RESPONSIBILITY by Sandra L. Bloom and Michael Reichert. (1998). "A totally convincing argument. . . . Demands careful study by all elected representatives, the clergy, the mental health and medical professions, representatives of the media, and all those unwittingly involved in this repressive perpetuation and catastrophic global problem." *Harold I. Eist, MD, Past President, American Psychiatric Association*

TREATING CHILDREN WITH SEXUALLY ABUSIVE BEHAVIOR PROB-LEMS: GUIDELINES FOR CHILD AND PARENT INTERVENTION by Jan Ellen Burton, Lucinda A. Rasmussen, Julie Bradshaw, Barbara J. Christopherson, and Steven C. Huke. (1998). "An extremely readable book that is well-documented and a mine of valuable 'hands on' information. . . . This is a book that all those who work with sexually abusive children or want to work with them must read." *Sharon K. Araji, PhD, Professor of Sociology, University of Alaska, Anchorage*

THE LEARNING ABOUT MYSELF (LAMS) PROGRAM FOR AT-RISK PARENTS: LEARNING FROM THE PAST—CHANGING THE FUTURE by Verna Rickard. (1998). "This program should be a part of the resource materials of every mental health professional trusted with the responsibility of working with 'at-risk' parents." *Terry King, PhD, Clinical Psychologist, Federal Bureau of Prisons, Catlettsburg, Kentucky*

THE LEARNING ABOUT MYSELF (LAMS) PROGRAM FOR AT-RISK PARENTS: HANDBOOK FOR GROUP PARTICIPANTS by Verna Rickard. (1998). "Not only is the LAMS program designed to be educational and build skills for future use, it is also fun!" *Martha Morrison Dore, PhD, Associate Professor of Social Work, Columbia University, New York, New York*

BRIDGING WORLDS: UNDERSTANDING AND FACILITATING ADOL-ESCENT RECOVERY FROM THE TRAUMA OF ABUSE by Joycee Kennedy and Carol McCarthy. (1998). "An extraordinary survey of the history of child neglect and abuse in America. . . . A wonderful teaching tool at the university level, but should be required reading in high schools as well." *Florabel Kinsler, PhD, BCD, LCSW, Licensed Clinical Social Worker, Los Angeles, California*

CEDAR HOUSE: A MODEL CHILD ABUSE TREATMENT PROGRAM by Bobbi Kendig with Clara Lowry. (1998). "Kendig and Lowry truly . . . realize the saying that we are our brothers' keepers. Their spirit permeates this volume, and that spirit of caring is what always makes the difference for people in painful situations." *Hershel K. Swinger, PhD, Clinical Director, Children's Institute International, Los Angeles, California*

SEXUAL, PHYSICAL, AND EMOTIONAL ABUSE IN OUT-OF-HOME CARE: PREVENTION SKILLS FOR AT-RISK CHILDREN by Toni Cavanagh Johnson and Associates. (1997). "Professionals who make dispositional decisions or who are related to out-of-home care for children could benefit from reading and following the curriculum of this book with children in placements." *Issues in Child Abuse Accusations*

Order Your Own Copy of
This Important Book for Your Personal Library!

WE ARE NOT ALONE
A Teenage Boy's Personal Account of Child Sexual Abuse from Disclosure Through Prosecution and Treatment

_____in softbound at $14.95 (ISBN: 0-7890-0927-7)

COST OF BOOKS_____

OUTSIDE USA/CANADA/
MEXICO: ADD 20%____

POSTAGE & HANDLING_____
*(US: $4.00 for first book & $1.50
for each additional book)
Outside US: $5.00 for first book
& $2.00 for each additional book)*

SUBTOTAL_____

in Canada: add 7% GST____

STATE TAX____
*(NY, OH & MIN residents, please
add appropriate local sales tax)*

FINAL TOTAL____
*(If paying in Canadian funds,
convert using the current
exchange rate, UNESCO
coupons welcome.)*

❏ **BILL ME LATER:** ($5 service charge will be added)
(Bill-me option is good on US/Canada/Mexico orders only;
not good to jobbers, wholesalers, or subscription agencies.)

❏ Check here if billing address is different from
shipping address and attach purchase order and
billing address information.

Signature_____

❏ **PAYMENT ENCLOSED: $_____**

❏ **PLEASE CHARGE TO MY CREDIT CARD.**

❏ Visa ❏ MasterCard ❏ AmEx ❏ Discover
❏ Diner's Club ❏ Eurocard ❏ JCB

Account # _____

Exp. Date_____

Signature_____

Prices in US dollars and subject to change without notice.

NAME_____

INSTITUTION_____

ADDRESS_____

CITY_____

STATE/ZIP_____

COUNTRY_____ COUNTY (NY residents only)_____

TEL_____ FAX_____

E-MAIL_____

May we use your e-mail address for confirmations and other types of information? ❏ Yes ❏ No
We appreciate receiving your e-mail address and fax number. Haworth would like to e-mail or fax special
discount offers to you, as a preferred customer. **We will never share, rent, or exchange your e-mail address
or fax number.** We regard such actions as an invasion of your privacy.

Order From Your Local Bookstore or Directly From
The Haworth Press, Inc.
10 Alice Street, Binghamton, New York 13904-1580 • USA
TELEPHONE: 1-800-HAWORTH (1-800-429-6784) / Outside US/Canada: (607) 722-5857
FAX: 1-800-895-0582 / Outside US/Canada: (607) 722-6362
E-mail: getinfo@haworthpressinc.com
PLEASE PHOTOCOPY THIS FORM FOR YOUR PERSONAL USE.
www.HaworthPress.com

BOF00

364.15   Angelica, Jade C.
Ang   (Jade Christine),
           1952-

         We are not alone.

DATE			